Monologues from Shakespeare's First Folio for Any Gender: *The Tragedies*

The Applause Shakespeare Monologue Series

Other Shakespeare Titles From Applause

Once More unto the Speech Dear Friends
Volume One: The Comedies
Compiled and Edited with Commentary by Neil Freeman

Once More unto the Speech Dear Friends
Volume Two: The Histories
Compiled and Edited with Commentary by Neil Freeman

Once More unto the Speech Dear Friends
Volume Three: The Tragedies
Compiled and Edited with Commentary by Neil Freeman

The Applause First Folio in Modern Type
Prepared and Annotated by Neil Freeman

The Folio Texts
Prepared and Annotated by Neil Freeman, Each of the 36 plays of the
Applause First Folio in Modern Type individually bound

The Applause Shakespeare Library
Plays of Shakespeare Edited for Performance

Soliloquy: The Shakespeare Monologues

Monologues from Shakespeare's First Folio for Any Gender:
The Tragedies

Compilation and Commentary by
Neil Freeman

Edited by
Paul Sugarman

APPLAUSE
THEATRE & CINEMA BOOKS
Guilford, Connecticut

APPLAUSE
THEATRE & CINEMA BOOKS

An imprint of Globe Pequot, the trade division of
The Rowman & Littlefield Publishing Group, Inc.
4501 Forbes Blvd., Ste. 200
Lanham, MD 20706
www.rowman.com

Distributed by NATIONAL BOOK NETWORK

Library of Congress Cataloging-in-Publication Data available

Library of Congress Control Number: 2021944382

ISBN 978-1-4930-5680-4 (paperback)
ISBN 978-1-4930-5681-1 (ebook)

Dedication

Although Neil Freeman passed to that "undiscovered country" in 2015, his work continues to lead students and actors to a deeper understanding of Shakespeare's plays. With the exception of Shakespeare's words (and my humble foreword), the entirety of the material within these pages is Neil's. May these editions serve as a lasting legacy to a life of dedicated scholarship, and a great passion for Shakespeare.

Contents

FOREWORD

Paul Sugarman

Monologues from Shakespeare's First Folio presents the work of Neil Freeman, longtime champion of Shakespeare's First Folio, whose groundbreaking explorations into how first printings offered insights to the text in rehearsals, stage and in the classroom. This work continued with *Once More Unto the Speech Dear Friends: Monologues from Shakespeare's First Folio with Modern Text Versions for Comparison* where Neil collected over 900 monologues divided between the Comedy, History and Tragedy Published by Applause in three masterful volumes which present the original First Folio text side by side with the modern, edited version of the text. These volumes provide a massive amount of material and information. However both the literary scope, and the literal size of these volumes can be intimidating and overwhelming. This series' intent is to make the work more accessible by taking material from the encyclopediac original volumes and presenting it in an accessible workbook format.

To better focus the work for actors and students the texts are contrasted side by side with introductory notes before and commentary after to aid the exploration of the text. By comparing modern and First Folio printings, Neil points the way to gain new insights into Shakespeare's text. Editors over the centuries have "corrected" and updated the texts to make them "accessible," or "grammatically correct." In doing so they have lost vital clues and information that Shakespeare placed there for his actors. With the texts side by side, you can see where and why editors have made changes and what may have been lost in translation.

In addition to being divided into Histories, Comedies, and Tragedies, the original series further breaks down speeches by the character's designated gender, also indicating speeches appropriate for any gender. Drawing from this example, this series breaks down each original volume into four workbooks: speeches for Women of all ages, Younger Men, Older Men and Any Gender. Gender is naturally fluid for Shakespeare's characters since during his time, ALL of the characters were portrayed by males. Contemporary productions of Shakespeare commonly switch character genders (Prospero has become Prospera), in addition to presenting single gender, reverse gender and gender non-specific productions. There are certainly characters and speeches where the gender is immaterial, hence the inclusion of a volume of speeches for Any Gender. This was something that Neil had indicated in the original volumes; we are merely following his example.

Once More Unto the Speech Dear Friends was a culmination of Neil's dedicated efforts to make the First Folio more accessible and available to readers and to illuminate for actors the many clues within the Folio text, as originally published. The material in this book is drawn from that work and retains Neil's British spelling of words (i.e. capitalisation) and his extensive commentary on each speech. Neil went on to continue this work as a master teacher of Shakespeare with another series of Shakespeare editions, his 'rhythm texts' and the ebook that he published on Apple Books, *The Shakespeare Variations.*

Neil published on his own First Folio editions of the plays in modern type which were the basis the Folio Texts series published by Applause of all 36 plays in the First Folio. These individual editions all have extensive notes on the changes that modern editions had made. This material was then combined to create a complete reproduction of the First Folio in modern type, *The Applause First Folio of Shakespeare in Modern Type.* These editions make the First Folio more accessible than ever before. The examples in this book demonstrate how the clues from the First Folio will give insights to understanding and performing these speeches and why it is a worthwhile endeavour to discover the riches in the First Folio.

PREFACE AND BRIEF BACKGROUND
TO THE FIRST FOLIO

WHY ANOTHER SERIES OF SOLILOQUY BOOKS?

There has been an enormous change in theatre organisation recent in the last twenty years. While the major large-scale companies have continued to flourish, many small theatre companies have come into being, leading to
- much doubling
- cross gender casting, with many one time male roles now being played legitimately by/as women in updated time-period productions
- young actors being asked to play leading roles at far earlier points in their careers

All this has meant actors should be able to demonstrate enormous flexibility rather than one limited range/style. In turn, this has meant
- a change in audition expectations
- actors are often expected to show more range than ever before
- often several shorter audition speeches are asked for instead of one or two longer ones
- sometimes the initial auditions are conducted in a shorter amount of time

Thus, to stay at the top of the game, the actor needs more knowledge of what makes the play tick, especially since
- early plays demand a different style from the later ones
- the four genres (comedy, history, tragedy, and the peculiar romances) all have different acting/textual requirements
- parts originally written for the older, more experienced actors again require a different approach from those written for the younger

ones, as the young roles, especially the female ones, were played by young actors extraordinarily skilled in the arts of rhetoric

There's now much more knowledge of how the original quarto and folio texts can add to the rehearsal exploration/acting and directing process as well as to the final performance.

Each speech is made up of four parts

- a background to the speech, placing it in the context of the play, and offering line length and an approximate timing to help you choose what might be right for any auditioning occasion
- a modern text version of the speech, with the sentence structure clearly delineated side by side with
- a folio version of the speech, where modern texts changes to the capitalization, spelling and sentence structure can be plainly seen
- a commentary explaining the differences between the two texts, and in what way the original setting can offer you more information to explore

Thus if they wish, **beginners** can explore just the background and the modern text version of the speech.

An actor experienced in exploring the Folio can make use of the background and the Folio version of the speech

And those wanting to know as many details as possible and how they could help define the deft stepping stones of the arc of the speech can use all four elements on the page.

The First Folio

(FOR LIST OF CURRENT REPRODUCTIONS SEE BIBLIOGRAPHY

The end of 1623 saw the publication of the justifiably famed First Folio (F1). The single volume, published in a run of approximately 1,000 copies at the princely sum of one pound (a tremendous risk, considering that a single play would sell at no more than six pence, one fortieth of F1's price, and that the annual salary of a schoolmaster was only ten pounds), contained thirty-six plays.

The manuscripts from which each F1 play would be printed came from a variety of sources. Some had already been printed. Some came from the playhouse complete with production details. Some had no theatrical input at all, but were handsomely copied out and easy to read. Some were supposedly very messy, complete with first draft scribbles and crossings out. Yet, as Charlton Hinman, the revered dean of First Folio studies describes F1 in the Introduction to the Norton Facsimile:

> It is of inestimable value for what it is, for what it contains. For here are preserved the masterworks of the man universally recognized as our greatest writer; and preserved, as Ben Jonson realized at the time of the original publication, not for an age but for all time.

WHAT DOES F1 REPRESENT?

- texts prepared for actors who rehearsed three days for a new play and one day for one already in the repertoire
- written in a style (rhetoric incorporating debate) so different from ours (grammatical) that many modern alterations based on grammar (or poetry) have done remarkable harm to the rhetorical/debate quality of the original text and thus to interpretations of characters at key moments of stress.
- written for an acting company the core of which steadily grew older, and whose skills and interests changed markedly over twenty years as well as for an audience whose make-up and interests likewise changed as the company grew more experienced

The whole is based upon supposedly the best documents available at the time, collected by men closest to Shakespeare throughout his career, and brought to a single printing house whose errors are now widely understood - far more than those of some of the printing houses that produced the original quartos.

TEXTUAL SOURCES FOR THE AUDITION SPEECHES

Individual modern editions consulted in the preparation of the Modern Text version of the speeches are listed in the Bibliography under the separate headings 'The Complete Works in Compendium Format' and ' The Complete Works in Separate Individual Volumes.' Most of the modern versions of the speeches are a compilation of several of these texts. However, all modern act, scene and/or line numbers refer the reader to The Riverside Shakespeare, in my opinion still the best of the complete works despite the excellent compendiums that have been published since.

The First Folio versions of the speeches are taken from a variety of already published sources, including not only all the texts listed in the 'Photostatted Reproductions in Compendium Format' section of the Bibliography, but also earlier, individually printed volumes, such as the twentieth century editions published under the collective title *The Facsimiles of Plays from The First Folio of Shakespeare* by Faber & Gwyer, and the nineteenth century editions published on behalf of The New Shakespeare Society.

INTRODUCTION

So, congratulations , you've got an audition, and for a Shakespeare play no less.

You've done all your homework, including, hopefully , reading the whole play to see the full range and development of the character.

You've got an idea of the character, the situation in which you/it finds itself (the given circumstance s); what your/its needs are (objectives/intentions); and what you intend to do about them (action /tactics).

You've looked up all the unusual words in a good dictionary or glossary; you've turned to a well edited modern edition to find out what some of the more obscure references mean.

And those of you who understand metre and rhythm have worked on the poetic values of the speech, and you are word perfect . . .

. . . and yet it's still not working properly and/or you feel there's more to be gleaned from the text , but you're not sure what that something is or how to go about getting at it; in other words, all is not quite right, yet.

THE KEY QUESTION

What text have you been working with - a good modern text or an 'original' text, that is a copy of one of the first printings of the play?

If it's a modern text, no matter how well edited (and there are some splendid single copy editions available, see the Bibliography for further details), despite all the learned information offered, it's not surprising you feel somewhat at a loss, for there is a huge difference between the original printings (the First Folio, and the individual quartos, see

Appendix 1 for further details) and any text prepared after 1700 right up to the most modern of editions. All the post 1700 texts have been tidied-up for the modern reader to ingest silently, revamped according to the rules of correct grammar, syntax and poetry. However the 'originals' were prepared for actors speaking aloud playing characters often in a great deal of emotional and/or intellectual stress, and were set down on paper according to the very flexible rules of rhetoric and a seemingly very cavalier attitude towards the rules of grammar, and syntax, and spelling, and capitalisation, and even poetry.

Unfortunately, because of the grammatical and syntactical standardisation in place by the early 1700's, many of the quirks and oddities of the origin also have been dismissed as 'accidental' - usually as compositor error either in deciphering the original manuscript, falling prey to their own particular idosyncracies, or not having calculated correctly the amount of space needed to set the text. Modern texts dismiss the possibility that these very quirks and oddities may be by Shakespeare, hearing his characters in as much difficulty as poor Peter Quince is in *A Midsummer Night's Dream* (when he, as the Prologue, terrified and struck down by stage fright, makes a huge grammatical hash in introducing his play 'Pyramus and Thisbe' before the aristocracy, whose acceptance or otherwise, can make or break him)

> If we offend, it is with our good will.
> That you should think, we come not to offend,
> But with good will.
> >   To show our simple skill,
> That is the true beginning of our end .
> Consider then, we come but in despite.
> We do not come, as minding to content you ,
> Our true intent is.
> >   All for your delight
> We are not here.
> >   That you should here repent you,

> The Actors are at hand; and by their show,
> You shall know all, that you are like to know.

(A Midsummer Night's Dream)

In many other cases in the complete works what was originally printed is equally 'peculiar,' but, unlike Peter Quince , these peculiarities are usually regularised by most modern texts.

However, this series of volumes is based on the belief - as the following will show - that most of these 'peculiarities' resulted from Shakespeare setting down for his actors the stresses, trials, and tribulations the characters are experiencing as they think and speak, and thus are theatrical gold-dust for the actor, director, scholar, teacher, and general reader alike.

THE FIRST ESSENTIAL DIFFERENCE BETWEEN THE TWO TEXTS

THINKING

A **modern** text can show

- the story line
- your character's conflict with the world at large
- your character's conflict with certain individuals within that world

but because of the very way an 'original' text was set, it can show you all this plus one key extra, the very thing that makes big speeches what they are

- the conflict within the character

WHY?

Any good playwright writes about characters in stressful situations who are often in a state of conflict not only with the world around them and the people in that world, but also within themselves. And you probably know from personal experience that when these conflicts occur people do not necessarily utter the most perfect of grammatical/poetic/ syntactic statements, phrases, or sentences. Joy and delight, pain and sorrow often come sweeping through in the way things are said, in the incoherence of the phrases, the running together of normally disassociated ideas, and even in the sounds of the words themselves.

The tremendous advantage of the period in which Shakespeare was setting his plays down on paper and how they first appeared in print was that when characters were rational and in control of self and situation, their phrasing and sentences (and poetic structure) would appear to be quite normal even to a modern eye - but when things were going wrong, so sentences and phrasing (and poetic structure) would become highly erratic. But the Quince type eccentricities are rarely allowed to stand. Sadly, in tidying , most modern texts usually make the text far too clean, thus setting rationality when none originally existed.

THE SECOND ESSENTIAL DIFFERENCE BETWEEN THE TWO TEXTS
SPEAKING, ARGUING, DEBATING

Having discovered what and how you/your character is thinking is only the first stage of the work - you/it then have to speak aloud, in a society that absolutely loved to speak - and not only speak ideas (content) but to speak entertainingly so as to keep listeners enthralled (and this was especially so when you have little content to offer and have to mask it somehow - think of today 's television adverts and political spin doctors as a parallel and you get the picture). Indeed one of the Elizabethan 'how to win an argument' books was very precise about this - George Puttenham, *The Art of English Poesie* (1589).

A: ELIZABETHAN SCHOOLING

All educated classes could debate/argue at the drop of a hat, for both boys (in 'petty-schools') and girls (by books and tutors) were trained in what was known overall as the art of rhetoric, which itself was split into three parts

- first, how to distinguish the real from false appearances/outward show (think of the three caskets in *The Merchant of Venice* where the language on the gold and silver caskets enticingly, and deceptively, seems to offer hopes of great personal rewards that are dashed when the language is carefully explored, whereas once the apparent threat on the lead casket is carefully analysed the reward therein is the greatest that could be hoped for)
- second, how to frame your argument on one of 'three great grounds'; honour/morality; justice/legality; and, when all else fails, expedience/ practicality.
- third, how to order and phrase your argument so winsomely that your audience will vote for you no matter how good the opposition - and there were well over two hundred rules and variations by which winning could be achieved, all of which had to be assimilated before a child's education was considered over and done with.

B: THINKING ON YOUR FEET: I.E. THE QUICK, DEFT , RAPID MODIFICATION OF EACH TINY THOUGHT

The Elizabethan/therefore your character/therefore you were also trained to explore and modify your thoughts as you spoke - never would you see a sentence in its entirety and have it perfectly worked out in your mind before you spoke (unless it was a deliberately written, formal public declaration, as with the Officer of the Court in The Winter' s Tale, reading the charges against Hermione). Thus after uttering your very first phrase, you might expand it, or modify it, deny it, change it, and so on throughout the whole sentence and speech.

Neil Freeman 23

From the poet Samuel Coleridge Taylor there is a wonderful description of how Shakespeare puts thoughts together like "a serpent twisting and untwisting in its own strength," that is, with one thought springing out of the one previous. Treat each new phrase as a fresh unravelling of the serpent's coil. What is discovered (and therefore said) is only revealed as the old coil/phrase disappears revealing a new coil in its place. The new coil is the new thought. The old coil moves/disappears because the previous phrase is finished with as soon as it is spoken.

C: MODERN APPLICATION

It is very rarely we speak dispassionately in our 'real' lives, after all thoughts give rise to feelings, feelings give rise to thoughts, and we usually speak both together - unless

1/ we're trying very hard for some reason to control ourselves and not give ourselves away

2/ or the volcano of emotions within us is so strong that we cannot control ourselves, and feelings swamp thoughts

3/ and sometimes whether deliberately or unconsciously we colour words according to our feelings; the humanity behind the words so revealed is instantly understandable.

D: HOW THE ORIGINAL TEXTS NATURALLY ENHANCE/ UNDERSCORE THIS CONTROL OR RELEASE

The amazing thing about the way all Elizabethan/early Jacobean texts were first set down (the term used to describe the printed words on the page being 'orthography'), is that it was flexible, it allowed for such variations to be automatically set down without fear of grammatical repercussion.

So if Shakespeare heard Juliet's nurse working hard to try to convince Juliet that the Prince's nephew Juliet is being forced to (bigamously) marry, instead of setting the everyday normal

'O he's a lovely gentleman'

which the modern texts HAVE to set, the first printings were permitted to set

'O hee's a Lovely Gentleman'

suggesting that something might be going on inside the Nurse that causes her to release such excessive extra energy.

E: BE CAREFUL

This needs to be stressed very carefully: the orthography doesn't dictate to you/force you to accept exactly what it means. The orthography simply suggests you might want to explore this moment further or more deeply.

In other words, simply because of the flexibility with which the Elizabethans/Shakespeare could set down on paper what they heard in their minds or wanted their listeners to hear, in addition to all the modern acting necessities of character - situation, objective, intention, action, and tactics the original Shakespeare texts offer pointers to where feelings (either emotional or intellectual, or when combined together as passion, both) are also evident.

SUMMARY

BASIC APPROACH TO THE SPEECHES SHOWN BELOW

(after reading the 'background')

1/ first use the modern version shown in the first column: by doing so you can discover

- the basic plot line of what's happening to the character, and
- the first set of conflicts/obstacles impinging on the character as a result of the situation or actions of other characters
- the supposed grammatical and poetical correctnesses of the speech

2/ then you can explore

- any acting techniques you'd apply to any modern soliloquy, including establishing for the character
- the given circumstances of the scene
- their outward state of being (who they are sociologically, etc.)
- their intentions and objectives
- the resultant action and tactics they decide to pursue

3/ when this is complete, turn to the First Folio version of the text, shown on the facing page: this will help you discover and explore

- the precise thinking and debating process so essential to an understanding of any Shakespeare text
- the moments when the text is NOT grammatically or poetically as correct as the modern texts would have you believe, which will in turn help you recognise
- the moments of conflict and struggle stemming from within the character itself
- the sense of fun and enjoyment the Shakespeare language nearly always offers you no matter how dire the situation

4/ should you wish to further explore even more the differences between the two texts, the commentary that follows discusses how the First Folio has been changed, and what those alterations might mean for the human arc of the speech

NOTES ON HOW THESE
SPEECHES ARE SET UP

For each of the speeches the first page will include the Background on the speech and other information including number of lines, approximate timing and who is addressed. Then will follow a spread which shows the modern text version on the left and the First Folio version on the right, followed by a page of Commentary.

PROBABLE TIMING: (shown on the Background page before the speeches begin, set below the number of lines) 0.45 = a forty-five second speech

SYMBOLS & ABBREVIATIONS IN THE COMMENTARY AND TEXT

F: the First Folio

mt.: modern texts

F # followed by a number: the number of the sentence under discussion in the First Folio version of the speech, thus F #7 would refer to the seventh sentence

mt. # followed by a numb er: the number of the sentence under discussion in the modern text version of the speech, thus mt. #5 would refer to the fifth sentence

/#, (e.g. 3/7): the first number refers to the number of capital letters in the passage under discussion; the second refers to the number of long spellings therein

within a quotation from the speech: / indicates where one verse line ends and a fresh one starts

[ ] : set around words in both texts when F1 sets one word , mt another

{ } : some minor alteration has been made, in a speech built up, where, a word or phrase will be changed, added, or removed

{†} : this symbol shows where a sizeable part of the text is omitted

TERMS FOUND IN THE COMMENTARY
OVERALL

1/ **orthography**: the capitalization, spellings, punctuation of the First Folio
SIGNS OF IMPORTANT DISCOVERIES/ARGUMENTS WITHIN A FIRST FOLIO SPEECH

2/ **major punctuation**: colons and semicolons: since the Shakespeare texts are based so much on the art of debate and argument, the importance of F1 's major punctuation must not be underestimated, for both the semi-colon (;) and colon (:) mark a moment of importance for the character, either for itself, as a moment of discovery or revelation, or as a key point in a discussion, argument or debate that it wishes to impress upon other characters onstage

as a rule of thumb:

a/ the more frequent colon (:) suggests that whatever the power of the point discovered or argued, the character is not side-tracked and can continue with the argument - as such, the colon can be regarded as a **logical** connection

b/ the far less frequent semicolon (;) suggests that because of the power inherent in the point discovered or argued, the character is side-tracked and momentarily loses the argument and falls back into itself or can only continue the argument with great difficulty - as such, the semicolon should be regarded as an **emotional** connection

3/ **surround phrases**: phrase(s) surrounded by major punctuation, or a combination of major punctuation and the end or beginning of a sentence: thus these phrases seem to be of especial importance for both character and speech, well worth exploring as key to the argument made and /or emotions released

DIALOGUE NOT FOUND IN THE FIRST FOLIO
∞ set where modern texts add dialogue from a quarto text which has not been included in Fl

A LOOSE RULE OF THUMB TO THE THINKING PROCESS OF A FIRST FOLIO CHARACTER

1/ mental discipline/**intellect**: a section where capitals dominate suggests that the intellectual reason ing behind what is being spoken or discovered is of more concern than the personal response beneath it

2/ feelings/**emotions**: a section where long spellings dominate suggests that the personal response to what is being spoken or discovered is of more concern than the intellectual reasoning behind it

3/ **passion**: a section where both long spellings and capitals are present in almost equal proportions suggests that both mind and emotion/feelings are inseparable, and thus the character is speaking passionately

SIGNS OF LESS THAN GRAMMATICAL THINKING WITHIN A FIRST FOLIO SPEECH

1/ **onrush:** sometimes thoughts are coming so fast that several topics are joined together as one long sentence suggesting that the F character's mind is working very quickly, or that his/her emotional state is causing some concern: most mod ern texts split such a sentence into several grammatically correct parts (the opening speech of *As You Like It* is a fine example, where F's long 18 line opening sentence is split into six): while the modern texts' resetting may be syntactically correct, the F moment is nowhere near as calm as the revisions suggest

2/ **fast-link:** sometimes F shows thoughts moving so quickly for a character that the connecting punctuation between disparate topics is merely a comma, suggesting that there is virtually no pause in springing from one idea to the next: unfortunately most modern texts rarely allow this to stand, instead replacing the obviously disturbed comma with a grammatical period, once more creating calm that it seems the original texts never intended to show

FIRST FOLIO SIGNS OF WHEN VERBAL GAME PLAYING HAS TO STOP

1/ **non-embellished:** a section with neither capitals nor long spellings suggests that what is being discovered or spoken is so important to the character that there is no time to guss it up with vocal or mental excesses: an unusual moment of self-control

2/ **short sentence:** coming out of a society where debate was second nature, man y of Shakespeare's characters speak in long sentences in which ideas are stated, explored, redefined and summarized all before moving onto the next idea in the argument, discovery or debate: the longer sentence is the sign of a rhetorically trained mind used to public speaking (oratory), but at times an idea or discovery is so startling or inevitable that length is either unnecessary or impossible to maintain : hence the occasional very important short sentence suggests that there is no time for the niceties of oratorical adornment with which to sugar the pill - verbal games are at an end and now the basic core of the issue must be faced

3/ **monosyllabic:** with English being composed of two strands, the polysyllabic (stemming from French, Italian, Latin and Greek), and the monosyllabic (from the Anglo-Saxon), each strand has two distinct functions: the polysyllabic words are often used when there is time for fanciful elaboration and rich description (which could be described as 'excessive rhetoric') while the monosyllabic occur when, literally, there is no other way of putting a basic question or comment - Juliet's "Do you love me? I know thou wilt say aye" is a classic example of both monosyllables and non-embellishment: with monosyllables, only the naked truth is being spoken, nothing is hidden

Monologues from Shakespeare's First Folio for Any Gender: *The Tragedies*

The Lamentable Tragedie of
Titus Andronicus

Marcus

Princes, that strive by Factions, and by Friends,
1.1.18 - 45

Background: the politician Marcus Andronicus, brother (perhaps younger) to Titus, responds to speeches of Saturninus and
Bassianus, informing the late emperor's sons of the people's choice

Style: public address in the open air to two men on behalf of all present

Where: unspecified, but a public square in Rome

To Whom: a large group, comprised of Tribunes, Senators, the emper-
or's two sons and their followers

# of Lines: 28

Probable Timing: 1.30 minutes

Take Note: F's public address oratory has been reduced by modern
text's jamming together F's sentences #4-#6: also F's orthography
adds much to the understanding of the speech.

Marcus

1   Princes, that strive by factions and by friends
     Ambitiously for rule and empery,
     Know, that the people of Rome, for whom we stand
     A special party, have by common voice,
     In election for the Roman empery,
     Chosen Andronicus, surnamed [Pius]
     For many good and great deserts to Rome.

2   A nobler man, a braver warrior,
     Lives not this day within the city walls .

3   He by the Senate is accited home
     From weary wars against the barbarous Goths,
     That with his sons, a terror to our foes,
     Hath yok'd a nation strong, train'd up in arms.

4   Ten years are spent, since first he undertook
     This cause of Rome, and chastised with arms
     Our enemies' pride; five times he hath return'd
     Bleeding to Rome, bearing his valiant sons
     In coffins from the field,
     And now at last, laden with honor's spoils,
     Returns the good Andronicus to Rome,
     Renowned Titus, flourishing in arms.

5   Let us entreat by honor of his name,
     Whom worthily you would have now succeed,
     And in the Capitol and Senate's right,
     Whom you pretend to honor and adore,
     That you withdraw you, and abate your strength,
     Dismiss your followers, and as suitors should,
     Plead your deserts in peace and humbleness.

Marcus

1 Princes, that strive by Factions, and by Friends,
  Ambitiously for Rule and Empery:
  Know, that the people of Rome for whom we stand
  A speciall Party, have by Common voyce
  In Election for the Romane Emperie,
  Chosen Andronicus, Sur-named [Pious],
  For many good and great deserts to Rome.

2 A Nobler man, a braver Warriour,
  Lives not this day within the City Walles.

3 He by the Senate is accited home
  From weary Warres against the barbarous Gothes,
       That with his Sonnes (a terror to our Foes
  Hath yoak'd a Nation strong, train'd up in Armes.

4 Ten yeares are spent, since first he undertooke
  This Cause of Rome, and chasticed with Armes
  Our Enemies pride.

5   Five times he hath return'd
  Bleeding to Rome, bearing his Valiant Sonnes
  In Coffins from the Field.

6 And now at last, laden with Honours Spoyles,
  Returnes the good Andronicus to Rome,
  Renowned Titus, flourishing in Armes.

7 Let us intreat, by Honour of his Name,
  Whom (worthily) you would have now succeede,
  And in the Capitoll and Senates right,
  Whom you pretend to Honour and Adore,
  That you withdraw you, and abate your Strength,
  Dismisse your Followers, and as Suters should,
  Pleade your Deserts in Peace and Humblenesse.

- with capitals outnumbering long spellings two to one (51/25) the speech is already a fine display of debate and precise argument

- this is even more enhanced when it's noted that 16 of the 25 long spellings are folded into words already capitalized – as if the force of the argument were giving rise to the accompanying personal release

- the colon at the end of the second line of F's first sentence has a fine 'announcing' quality to it ("now I have your attention, listen to what I'm going to say next"): modern texts completely wipe this out by replacing the colon with a comma

- the three separate F sentences #4-#6 allow Marcus to emphasise three separate points about his brother's accomplishments,viz.

    a/ the number of years he has served
    b/ how many times he lost his sons
    c/ the fact that he has now brought great wealth to Rome

   with far more impact than the modern texts resetting of the whole as one eight line sentence

The Lamentable Tragedie of Titus Andronicus

Aaron

'Twill vexe thy soule to heare what I shall speake :
between 5.1.62 - 85

Background: the following are two speeches of defiance by the captured Aaron: This speech is triggered by the fact Aaron's offer to speak on the guarantee his son's life will be spared is met with Lucius' reply 'if it please me which thou speak'st,/Thy child shall live, and I will see it nourisht', moving on to explain the pedigree of the child, and then quickly elaborating in full his own and Tamora's role in the destruction of all the Andronici, Lucius' family.

Style: address to one man in front of a large group

Where: on the road to Rome

To Whom: to Lucius, in front of the army of the Goths,

# of Lines: 19

Probable Timing: 1.00 minutes

Take Note: F's orthography opens up some quite surprising swings in mood and attitude not easily seen in the modern texts, all of which suggest several complex layers all vying for release, not just the ravings of a one dimensional figure of evil.

Aaron

1 'Twill vex thy soul to hear what I shall speak :
   For I must talk of [murders], rapes, and massacres,
   Acts of black night, abominable deeds,
   Complots of mischief , treason, villainies
   Ruthful to hear, yet piteously [perform'd] .

2 And this shall all be buried [in] my death,
   Unless thou swear to me my child shall live .

---

3 {†}   I know thou art religious,
   And hast a thing within thee called conscience,
   With twenty popish tricks and ceremonies,
   Which I have seen thee careful to observe,
   Therefore I urge thy oath ; for that I know
   An idiot holds his bauble for a god,
   And keeps the oath which by that god he swears,
   To that I'll urge him : therefore thou shalt vow
   By that same god, what god so'er it be
   That thou adorest and hast in reverence,
   To save my boy, to nourish and bring him up,
   Or else I will discover nought to thee .

Aaron

1   'Twill vexe thy soule to heare what I shall speake :
For I must talke of [Murthers], Rapes, and Massacres,
Acts of Blacke-night, abhominable Deeds,
Complots of Mischiefe, Treason, Villanies
Ruthfull to heare, yet pittiously [preform'd],
And this shall all be buried [by] my death,
Unlesse thou sweare to me my Childe shall live .

---

2   {†}   I know thou art Religious,
And hast a thing within thee, called Conscience,
With twenty Popish trickes and Ceremonies,
Which I have seene thee carefull to observe :
Therefore I urge thy oath, for that I know
An Ideot holds his Bauble for a God,
And keepes the oath which by that God he sweares,
To that Ile urge him : therefore thou shalt vow
By that same God, what God so ere it be
That thou adorest, and hast in reverence,
To save my Boy, to nourish and bring him up,
Or else I will discover nought to thee .

- the opening line is ferocious in its emotional release (0/4)

- the next three lines are full of intellectual savagery (8/3)

- and then as the tantalizing blackmail finishes the longer F opening sentence ("let my child live and I'll tell you") Aaron's personal needs come sweeping through (1/5), and the only other *passionate* release (capitals and long-spellings virtually matching) comes in the two lines of the incredibly insulting attack on Lucius' supposed religious beliefs (4/3 in just the two lines 6-7 of F #2)

- for the rest of the speech, either an intellectual self-control is maintained (the opening three lines of F #2 as the question of religion is broached, 4/1) or the last four lines of the speech demanding Lucius vow to save the child (3/0), or, and even more dangerously, . . .

- and at times, for the listeners, there are moments of very frightening non-embellished calm when Aaron is at his most demanding or incisive

    "And this shall all be buried by my death,"

    "Therefore I urge thy oath"

    "to nourish and bring him up,/Or else I will discover nought to thee"

The Lamentable Tragedie of Titus Andronicus

Aaron

{I am sorry} that I had not done a thousand more :
5.1.124 - 144

Background: Aaron in this speech rejects any form of regret for what he has done

Style: address to one man in front of a large group

Where: on the road to Rome

To Whom: to Lucius, in front of the army of the Goths,

# of Lines: 21

Probable Timing: 1.10 minutes

Take Note: The passion of the previous speech is just as marked here (15/21 in twenty-one lines), yet the switches are far more rapid and concentrated in smaller bursts than before.

Aaron

1   {I am sorry} that I had not done a thousand more.

2   Even now I curse the day, - and yet I think
      Few come within [the] compass of my curse -
      Wherein I did not some notorious ill :
      As kill a man, or else devise his death,
      Ravish a maid, or plot the way to do it,
      Accuse some innocent, and forswear myself,
      Set deadly enmity between two friends,
      Make poor men's cattle break their necks,
      Set fire on barns and haystacks in the night,
      And bid the owners quench them with [their] tears.

3   Oft have I digg'd up dead men from their graves,
      And set them upright at their dear friends door,
      Even when their sorrows almost was forgot,
      And on their skins, as on the bark of trees,
      Have with my knife carved in Roman letters,
      "Let not your sorrow die, though I am dead."

4   [But], I have done a thousand dreadful things,
      As willingly, as one would kill a fly,
      And nothing grieves me heartily indeed,
      But that I cannot do ten thousand more.

Aaron

1   {I am sorry} that I had not done a thousand more :
     Even now I curse the day, and yet I thinke
     Few come within [few] compasse of my curse,
     Wherein I did not some Notorious ill,
     As kill a man, or else devise his death,
     Ravish a Maid, or plot the way to do it,
     Accuse some Innocent, and forsweare my selfe,
     Set deadly Enmity betweene two Friends,
     Make poore mens Cattell breake their neckes,
     Set fire on Barnes and Haystackes in the night,
     And bid the Owners quench them with [the] teares :
     Oft have I dig'd up dead men from their graves,
     And set them upright at their deere Friends doore,
     Even when their sorrowes almost was forgot,
     And on their skinnes, as on the Barke of Trees,
     Have with my knife carved in Romaine Letters,
     Let not your sorrow die, though I am dead .

2   [Tut], I have done a thousand dreadfull things
     As willingly, as one would kill a Fly,
     And nothing greeves me hartily indeede,
     But that I cannot doe ten thousand more .

• it's interesting to see the utter calm of the opening line quickly moves into a much longer F sentence #1 where the remaining non-embellished lines, involving truly horrific images, viz.

> "{I am sorry} that I had not done a thousand more"
>
> "As kill a man, or else devise his death,"
>
> "Oft have I dig'd up dead men from their graves"
>
> "Let not your sorrow die, though I am dead"

divide the sentence into at least four different rhetorical parts each with their own speaking energy

• the bulk of the capitals fall into two particularly vicious clusters: more than half (8) in just 6 lines as Aaron begins to elaborate his attacks on the vulnerable, starting with 'Ravish a Maid' (starting line 5 F sentence #1), and 4 in the two lines describing what he would do with dead bodies he dug up (next to the last two lines of F #1)

• and the long spellings also fall into two patterns, either

a/ in clusters, as with 6 in two lines in the following
> "Make poore mens Cattell breake their neckes,
>
> Set fire on Barnes and Haystackes in the night," &
>
> "foresweare my selfe"

b/ often at the end of lines or phrases, as if the act of speaking leads to greater release as an idea is concluded/pushed home

The Tragedie of Romeo and Juliet
Chorus/Corus

Two households both alike in dignitie,
Prologue 1 – 14

Background: the opening to the play (as set in the second quarto, and omitted by the folio)

Style: a self explanatory introduction to the play, set in the form of a sonnet

Where: the theatre

To Whom: direct audience address

# of Lines: 14

Probable Timing: 0.45 minutes

Take Note: Written as a sonnet, the story is told emotionally (5/15) in four sections, (introduction/ complications/crisis/summary - the first three sections being four lines each, the last set two), yet the build of the two texts is very different. Most modern texts on-rush the end of the speech, mt. #3 combining the crisis and summary, whereas F gains control by the end of the speech, after an onrushed difficult to control start - F #1 combining together the introduction and the complications. Therefore it's not surprising most of F's releases come in the middle of it's onrushed first sentence.

The Prologue
Chorus

1   Two households, both alike in dignity ,
     In fair Verona, where we lay our scene
     From ancient grudge, break to new mutiny,
     Where civil blood makes civil hands unclean .

2   From forth the fatal loins of these two foes,
     A pair of star-cross'd lovers take their life ;
     Whose misadventur'd piteous overthrows
     Doth with their death bury their parents' strife .

3   The fearful passage of their death-mark'd love,
     And the continuance of their parents' rage,
     Which, but their children's end, nought could remove,
     Is now the two hours traffic of our stage ;
     The which if you with patient ears attend,
     What here shall miss, our toil shall strive to mend .

The Prologue
Corus

1   Two households both alike in dignitie,
      (In faire Verona where we lay our Scene)
      From auncient grudge, breake to new mutinie,
      Where civill bloud makes civill hands uncleane :
      From forth the fatall loynes of these two foes,
      A paire of starre-crost lovers, take their life :
      Whose misadventur'd pittious overthrowes,
      Doth with their death burie theur Parents strife .

2   The fearfull passage of their death-markt love,
      And the continuance of their Parents rage :
      Which but their childrens end nought could remove :
      Is now the two houres trafficque of our Stage .

3   The which if you with patient eares attend,
      What heare shall misse, our toyle shall strive to mend .

the Prologue, though set in Q1-4, was not printed in F1: the text
   here is taken from Q2

• however, the speech opens calmly, with an unembellished first line (perhaps the ensuing story is difficult to share, with the final word 'dignitie' being short spelled)

• but even as the second line establishes the locale so the releases start (2/1), and then, spilling over the break between introduction and summary, the information of the 'ancient grudge' leading eventually to the fate of the 'paire of starre-crost lovers' is expressed via an enormous emotional release (0/10 in just four lines): and once their deaths have been spoken of, the Chorus seems to regain self-control, for the acknowledgement that their 'death burie theur Parents strife' is mildly factual and emotional (1/1, the last two lines of F #1)

• in comparison to the start of the speech, F #2's explanation that the story will be 'the two houres trafficque of our Stage' seems fairly relaxed (2/3) initially, yet the fact that this is the crisis section of the sonnet and the last two lines are expressed as surround phrases suggests that the Chorus might be working very hard to keep the appearance of control – fear of audience response perhaps – especially since the F #3 summary appealing that 'patient eares attend' is so emotional (0/4 in just two lines)

The Tragedie of Romeo and Juliet
Prince

Rebellious Subjects, Enemies to peace,
1.1.81 - 103

Background: the ongoing quarrel between the two houses of Capulet and Mountague has lead to further street brawls involving innocent and angry citizens: this is their Prince's first on-stage attempt to prevent matters growing further out of hand

Style: group address in the open air

Where: public street

To Whom: the Capulets, including the head of the family, his wife and hot-headed nephew Tybalt; the Mountagues, including the head of the family, his wife and hot-headed nephew Benvolio; citizens at large and members of the watch

# of Lines: 23

Probable Timing: 1.10 minutes

Take Note: F's orthography suggests the Prince has great personal difficulty in quieting the disturbance, while the final onrushed F #4 (split into three by most modern texts) suggests even though by F #3 he seems to have established self-control, in his final series of commands and warnings his control begins to slip once more.

Prince

1   Rebellious subjects, enemies to peace,
    Profaners of this neighbor-stained steel -
    Will they not hear? -

2   What ho, you men, you beasts!
    That quench the fire of your pernicious rage
    With purple fountains issuing from your veins-
    On pain of torture, from those bloody hands
    Throw your mistempered weapons to the ground,
    And hear the sentence of your moved prince.

3   Three civil [brawls], bred of an airy word,
    By thee, old Capulet, and [Montague],
    Have thrice disturb'd the quiet of our streets,
    And made Verona's ancient citizens
    Cast by their grave beseeming ornaments
    To wield old partisans, in hands as old,
    Cank'red with peace, to part your cank'red hate ;
    If ever you disturb our streets again,
    Your lives shall pay the forfeit of the peace.

4   For this time all the rest depart away.

6   You, Capulet, shall go along with me,
    And, [Montague], come you this afternoon,
    To know our [farther] pleasure in this case,
    To old Free-town, our common judgment-place.

7   Once more, on pain of death, all men depart

Prince

1 Rebellious Subjects, Enemies to peace,
   Prophaners of this Neighbor-stained Steele,
   Will they not heare?

2   What hoe, you Men, you Beasts,
   That quench the fire of your pernitious Rage,
   With purple Fountaines issuing from your Veines:
   On paine of Torture, from those bloody hands
   Throw your mistemper'd Weapons to the ground,
   And heare the Sentence of your mooved Prince.

3 Three civill [Broyles], bred of an Ayery word,
   By thee old Capulet and [Mountague],
   Have thrice disturb'd the quiet of our streets,
   And made Verona's ancient Citizens
   Cast by their Grave beseeming Ornaments,
   To wield old Partizans, in hands as old,
   Cankred with peace, to part your Cankred hate,
   If ever you disturbe our streets againe,
   Your lives shall pay the forfeit of the peace.

4 For this time all the rest depart away:
   You Capulet shall goe along with me,
   And [Mountague] come you this afternoone,
   To know our [Fathers] pleasure in this case:
   To old Free-towne, our common judgement place:
   Once more on paine of death, all men depart.

• given the circumstances it's not surprising the unembellished lines are few and far between, the horror of civil chaos resulting in

'Have thrice disturb'd the quiet of our streets,"

plus the seriousness of

"Your lives shall pay the forfeit of the peace .

For this time all the rest depart away : "

the latter doubly weighted by being one of only two surround phrases in the speech

• the fact that Mountague and Capulet must report for hearings

" : To old Free-towne, our common judgement place : "

is set as a surround phrase might well suggest that a 'common judgement place' is not where two such worthies might expect to be summoned, and therefore could be construed as deliberate humiliation

• the initial (unsuccessful) command for attention is passionate (F #1, 4/3)

• to be followed by an equally unsuccessful intellectual attempt to shame them as 'Beasts' (the opening two and half lines of F #2, 5/2), while the last three lines, resorting to the threat of 'Torture' and the identifying this as the third of 'civill Broyles, bred of an Ayery word,' becomes passionate once more (6/6, the last three lines of F #2, and the first of F #3)

• and having got their attention,, it seems the Prince has regained public and private control, at least for F #3's next six very factual lines describing the result of these 'Broyles' (8/0), only to become emotional on the warning 'If ever you disturbe our streets againe," (0/2), followed by the two unembellished lines discussed above

• and control fades away throughout the onrushed F #4, the three lines telling the heads of the families they will soon learn the Prince's 'pleasure in this case' being passionate (3/3), and the last two, with the potential insult of where 'judgement' will be pronounced and a further command on 'paine of death' for 'all men' to 'depart' turning purely emotional (0/3)

The Tragedie of Romeo and Juliet

Chorus

Now old desire doth in his death bed lie,
Act Two Chorus 1 - 14

Background: a short speech of plot advancement following the first
meeting of Romeo and Juliet at the Capulet party

Style: a self explanatory speech set in the form of a sonnet

Where: the theatre

To Whom: direct audience address

# of Lines: 14

Probable Timing: 0.45 minutes

Take Note: Once more set as a sonnet, most modern texts present a
totally normal (4/4/4/2) linear structure. However, after a calm
start – the unembellished opening two lines hinting at a new love
– F moves into passion as the audience is told Rosaline is 'now not
faire' when compared with Juliet (2/2 F #1's last two lines). And
then, unlike the modern texts' continued rationality, F's remaining ten lines are totally onrushed, and, overall, full of passionate
release (11/16). Interestingly most of the emotional releases come
at the end of each line, implying a certain rhetorical flourish as
the information unfolds.

Chorus

1   Now old desire doth in his death bed lie,
    And young affection gapes to be his heir;
    That fair, for which Love groan'd for, and would die,
    With tender Juliet match'd, is now not fair .

2   Now Romeo is beloved, and loves again,
    [Alike] bewitched by the charm of looks ;
    But to his foe suppos'd he must complain,
    And she steal love's sweet bait from fearful hooks !

3   Being held a foe, he may not have access
    To breathe such vows as lovers use to swear;
    And she as much in love, her means much less
    To meet her new-beloved any where .

4   But passion lends them power, time means, to meet,
    Temp'ring extremities with extreme sweet .

Chorus

1   Now old desire doth in his death bed lie,
     And yong affection gapes to be his Heire,
     That faire, for which Love gron'd for and would die,
     With tender Juliet matcht, is now not faire .

2   Now Romeo is beloved, and Loves againe,
     [A like] bewitched by the charme of lookes :
     But to his foe suppos'd he must complaine,
     And she steale Loves sweet bait from fearefull hookes :
     Being held a foe, he may not have accesse
     To breath such vowes as Lovers use to sweare,
     And she as much in Love, her meanes much lesse,
     To meet her new Beloved any where :
     But passion lends them Power, time, meanes to meete,
     Temp'ring extremities with extreame sweete .

- thus as the complications section starts, F 2's first line, 'Romeo is beloved', is informatively passionate (2/1), but, wonderfully, the remaining three lines of the section, both characters being 'bewitched' are highly emotional (1/6), and thus rushes straight into . . .

- . . . the dilemma of their being unable to meet as normal lovers, (because of their parents' enmity a worthy subject for a crisis section), while still described passionately (3/5), each time 'love' is mentioned it is capitalised ('Lovers', 'Love', and 'Beloved'), which in turn rushes into the summary

- . . . explaining their 'passion' creates 'meanes to meete' – the accompanying emotion (1/4 in just two lines) perhaps suggesting the Chorus is anticipating the bitter-sweet that is to follow

The Tragedie of Romeo and Juliet
Frier Lawrence
Holy S Francis, what a change is heere ?
2.3.65 - 80

Background: having been told of Romeo's new found love for Juliet, and his insistence 'That thou consent to marrie us to day', Frier Lawrence is rightfully somewhat skeptical

Style: as part of a two-handed scene

Where: somewhere in the fields close to his cell

To Whom: Romeo

# of Lines: 16

Probable Timing: 0.50 minutes

Take Note: In addition to the obvious passion, most modern texts seem to present quite an emphatic Frier too (exclamation points ending mt. #1, #4 and #5 instead of F's question marks, and a co-lon ending the first line of mt's #9 instead of F's comma), whereas F seems to suggest a man who while occasionally exasperated (the enormously emotional - and humourous? - F #5, 1/8 in just four lines) is one who attempts to deal with Romeo rationally as well.

Frier Lawrence

1   Holy [Saint] Francis, what a change is here !

2   Is Rosaline, that thou didst love so dear,
     So soon forsaken ?

3   Young men's love then lies
     Not truly in their hearts, but in their eyes .

4   Jesu Maria, what a deal of brine
     Hath wash'd thy sallow cheeks for Rosaline !

5   How much salt water thrown away in waste,
     To season love, that of it doth not taste !

6   The sun nor yet thy sighs from heaven clears,
     Thy old groans yet ringing in my ancient ears;
     Lo here upon thy cheek the stain doth sit
     Of an old tear that is not wash'd off yet .

7   If e'er thou wast thyself and these woes thine,
     Thou and these woes were all for Rosaline .

8   And art thou chang'd ?

9   Pronounce this sentence then :
     Women may fall, when there's no strength in men.

Frier Lawrence

1   Holy [S] Francis, what a change is heere?

2   Is Rosaline that thou didst Love so deare
     So soone forsaken ? young mens Love then lies
     Not truely in their hearts, but in their eyes .

3   Jesu Maria what a deale of brine
     Hath washt thy sallow cheekes for Rosaline ?

4   How much salt water throwne away in wast,
     To season Love that of it doth not tast .

5   The Sun nor yet thy sighes, from heaven cleares,
     Thy old grones yet ringingin my auncient eares :
     Lo here upon thy cheeke the staine doth sit,
     Of an old teare that is not washt off yet .

6   If ere thou wast thy selfe, and these woes thine,
     Thou and these woes, were all for Rosaline .

7   And art thou chang'd ? pronounce this sentence then,
     Women may fall, when there's no strength in men .

- in no way does this rationality dismiss the Frier's sense of mocking humour, as the passionate (3/3) surround lines forming F #2 suggest

  ". Is Rosaline that thou didst Love so deare/So soone forsaken? young mens Love then lies/Not truely in their hearts, but in their eyes ."

- and while the speech ending maxim seems quite serious in its unembellishment

  " . And art thou chang'd? pronounce this sentence then,/Women may fall, when there's no strength in men . "

the fact that it is also made up of (two) surround phrases suggests the Frier may be having some quiet fun too

- in the opening surprise and the first questioning/mocking of Romeo's tears for Rosaline, the speech starts passionately (8/7 in the eight lines F #1-4)

- then comes the enormous emotional release as the Frier reaches the climax to his mocking of Romeo's earlier mooning over Rosaline (F #5, 1/8)

- and then the Frier becomes much more controlled, with the mock, if still there rather than a rebuke, first vastly reduced in terms of release, (1/1, F #6), and he finishes without any release at all (F #7)

The Tragedie of Romeo and Juliet

Benvolio

{Tybalt} began this [ ] Fray ,
3.1.151 - 175

Background: as a result of the challenge two young people have
died: Tybalt has killed Mercutio (who was in part defending Romeo's honour after Romeo, newly married to Tybalt's cousin Juliet, had refused to fight): in revenge a distraught Romeo has
killed Tybalt: since the Capulet Tybalt was killed by the Mountague Romeo, they are now demanding Romeo's death and, before giving judgement, the Prince has demanded of Benvolio 'who
began this Fray?': this is Benvolio's answer, his final words in the
play

Style: public address to one person, in front of a large group

Where: public street

To Whom: the Prince, in front of the Capulets, including the head
of the family and his wife; the Mountagues, including the head of
the family and his wife; citizens at large and members of the
watch

# of Lines: 25

Probable Timing: 1.15 minutes

Take: Note Including the proper names that open the first two lines,
Benvolio's attempt to maintain self-control lasts just two lines
(4/1).

Benvolio

1   {†}   {Tybalt} began this [bloody] fray {,}
     Tybalt, here slain, whom Romeo's hand did slay !

2   Romeo that spoke him fair, bid him bethink
     How nice the quarrel was, and urg'd withal
     Your high displeasure ; all this, uttered
     With gentle breath, calm look, knees humbly bow'd,
     Could not take truce with the unruly spleen
     Of [Tybalt] deaf to peace, but that he tilts
     With piercing steel at bold Mercutio's breast,
     Who, all as hot, turns deadly point to point,
     And, with a martial scorn, with one hand beats
     Cold death aside, and with the other sends
     It back to Tybalt, whose dexterity
     Retorts it .

3   Romeo he cries aloud,
     "Hold friends! friends part!" and swifter [than]his tongue,
     His [agile] arm beats down their fatal points,
     And 'twixt them rushes; underneath whose arm
     An envious thrust from Tybalt hit the life
     Of stout Mercutio, and then Tybalt fled ;
     But by and by comes back to Romeo,
     Who had but newly entertained Revenge,
     And to't they go like lightning, for, ere I
     Could draw to part them, was stout Tybalt slain;
     And as he fell, did Romeo turn and fly.

4   This is the truth, or let Benvolio die.

Benvolio

1   {†}   {Tybalt} began this [ ] Fray {,}
    Tybalt here slaine, whom Romeo's hand did slay,
    Romeo that spoke him faire, bid him bethinke
    How nice the Quarrell was, and urg'd withall
    Your high displeasure : all this uttered,
    With gentle breath, calme looke, knees humbly bow'd
    Could not take truce with the unruly spleene
    Of [Tybalts] deafe to peace, but that he Tilts
    With Peircing steele at bold Mercutio's breast,
    Who all as hot, turnes deadly point to point,
    And with a Martiall scorne, with one hand beates
    Cold death aside, and with the other sends
    It back to Tybalt, whose dexterity
    Retorts it : Romeo he cries aloud,
    Hold Friends, Friends part, and swifter [then] his tongue,
    His [aged] arme beats downe their fatall points,
    And twixt them rushes, underneath whose arme,
    An envious thrust from Tybalt, hit the life
    Of stout Mercutio, and then Tybalt fled .

2   But by and by comes backe to Romeo,
    Who had but newly entertained Revenge,
    And too't they goe like lightning, for ere I
    Could draw to part them, was stout Tybalt slaine :
    And as he fell, did Romeo turne and flie :
    This is the truth, or let Benvolio die .

- the next four lines attempting to assure the Prince of Romeo's 'faire' behaviour is very emotional (1/6), until reaching Tybalt's return

- his description of the fight, placing the blame on Tybalt (with his 'unruly spleen') and exonerating Mercutio ('with a Martiall scorne'), becomes passionate (5/6, the seven lines to the second colon – where mt. #2 ends)

- F's onrush into what happened next suggests Benvolio is very much caught up in the events he is reporting, and much less in control than the modern texts (which set a new sentence here) would suggest,

- thus the one and half line reporting of Romeo's words (F's equivalent to the start of mt. #3) becomes factual once more, (3/0) emphasising his peace-making appeal for them to act as 'Friends', which immediately turns emotional as Benvolio describes Romeo's coming between the combatants to beat 'downe their fatall points' (0/4 in just two lines)

- the description of Tybalt's actions, striking Mercutio, fleeing, and returning to face Romeo becomes strongly factual once more (5/1 the last two lines of F #1 and the first two of F #2) as if Benvolio once more were laying all the blame on Tybalt

- the ensuing fight and killing of Tybalt is described passionately (2/3)

- and at last with Tybalt's death, Romeo's flight and Benvolio's offer to 'die' if what he has just reported is not 'truth, come the only surround lines in the speech

    " : And as he fell, did Romeo turne and flie : / This is the truth, or let Benvolio die. "
    the final three lines being monosyllabic - save for the three proper names would suggest that the images are seemingly burnt into Benvolio's mind,

- the last line, 'the truth . . . or die' being unembellished - save for the capitalisation of his own name – suggests a very careful offer indeed, one with no time for extravagant images or justifications

The Tragedie of Romeo and Juliet

Prince

Seale up the mouth of outrage for a while,
three parts of 5.3: 216 - 221 291 - 295 305 - 310

Background: the final words of the play, preceded by a single line and then another sentence from an earlier part of the scene (sentences #1-2 as the speech now stands): two notes, 'your hate' refers to both houses, Capulet and Mountague, alike; the loss of a 'brace of Kinsmen' refers to his now dead nephews Mercutio and Paris

Style: general address

Where: at the opened Capulet Monument

To Whom: Juliet's two Capulet parents, Romeo's Mountague father, Frier Lawrence, members of the watch, and the pages to both Romeo and Paris, in front of the dead bodies of Romeo, Juliet, Paris, and the already shrouded Tybalt

# of Lines: 17

Probable Timing: 0.55 minutes

Prince

1   Seal up the mouth of outrage for a while,
     Till we can clear these ambiguities,
     And know their spring, their head, their true descent,
     And then will I be general of your woes,
     And lead you even to death.

2   Mean time forbear,
     And let mischance be slave to patience.

---

3   Where be these enemies?

4   Capulet!

5   Montague!

6   See what a scourge is laid upon your hate,
     That heaven finds means to kill your joys with love.

7   And I, for winking at your discords too
     Have lost a brace of kinsmen.

8   All are punish'd.

---

9   A [gloomy] peace this morning with it brings,
     The sun, for sorrow, will not show his head.

10   Go hence to have more talk of these sad things;
     Some shall be pardon'd, and some punished:
     For never was a story of more woe
     [Than] this of Juliet and her Romeo.

Prince

1   Seale up the mouth of outrage for a while,
    Till we can cleare these ambiguities,
    And know their spring, their head, their true descent,
    And then will I be generall of your woes,
    And lead you even to death? meane time forbeare,
    And let mischance be slave to patience,

2   Where be these Enemies?

3   Capulet, Montague,
    See what a scourge is laide upon your hate,
    That Heaven finds meanes to kill your joyes with Love ;
    And I, for winking at your discords too,
    Have lost a brace of Kinsmen : All are punish'd .

4   A [glooming] peace this morning with it brings,
    The Sunne for sorrow will not shew his head ;
    Go hence, to have more talke of these sad things,
    Some shall be pardon'd, and some punished .

5   For never was a Storie of more Wo,
    [Then] this of Juliet, and her Romeo .

• that the Prince is having difficulty maintaining self-control can be seen in

a/ the emotional opening (F #1, 0/5)

b/ the ungrammatical fast link connection via the question mark in line five jumping from shared grief with the instruction for 'patience' (where most modern texts create mt. #2)

c/ the onrush of F #3 (split into five sentences by most modern texts) where he speaks of the losses both families and he have suffered

• however, while F #3 is onrushed it is at least it is intellectually based (6/2) suggesting the Prince is struggling hard to present the facts as best as he can

• the constant return to unembellished moments

'And know their spring, their head, their true descent,'

'And let mischance be slave to patience'

'A glooming peace this morning with it brings,'

'And I, for winking at your discords too,'

'Some shall be pardon'd, and some punished.'

suggest an exhausted man constantly needing a moment (either of rest, or to calm himself) before he can continue

• this lack of energy most affects F #4's 'glooming' assessment of the forthcoming day (1/2 in four lines)

• though the Prince manages to gather enough mental energy to make the final summation of the overall tragedy (F #5, 4/0)

The Tragedie of Julius Cæsar

Murellus

Wherefore rejoyce?/What Conquest brings he home?

1.1.32 - 55

Background: At the top of the play, Cæsar has returned to Rome in triumph after defeating Pompey. The citizens have been given a holiday, to the disgust of two pro-Pompey supporters Flavius and Murellus who in their anguish not only remove laurel wreaths of victory from Cæsar's statuary (for which they are later executed), but, as here, berate the general citizenry in the midst of their celebrations.

Style: general address to a large group, initially via one man

Where: a public street

To Whom: initially the Cobbler, in front of Flavius, and citizens

# of Lines: 23

Probable Timing: 1.10 minutes

Take Note: The opening of two short sentences suggests a Murellus almost at a loss for words, while the peculiar and very ungrammatical setting of F #4 through to the opening of F #6 points to a reckless character, one not in full control of himself or his rhetoric: most modern texts set the much more grammatical three sentences as shown, establishing a sense of self-control that hardly matches his offstage foolhardiness in desecrating Caesar's images by removing the scarves that adorned them. The shading illustrates the enormous punctuation differences.

Murellus

1 Wherefore rejoice?

2   What conquest brings he home?

3 What tributaries follow him to Rome,
To grace in captive bonds his chariot-wheels?

4 You blocks, you stones, you worse [than] senseless things!

5 O you hard hearts, you cruel men of Rome,
Knew you not Pompey ?

6   Many a time and oft
Have you climb'd up to walls and battlements,
To tow'rs and windows, yea, to chimney-tops,
Your infants in your arms, and there have sate
The livelong day, with patient expectation,
To see great Pompey pass the streets of Rome ;
And when you saw his chariot but appear,
Have you not made an universal shout,
That [Tiber] trembled underneath her banks
To hear the replication of your sounds
Made in her concave shores?

7 And do you now put on your best attire?

8 And do you now cull out a holiday?

9 And do you now strew flowers in his way,
That comes in triumph over Pompey's blood?

10 Be gone !

11 Run to your houses, fall upon your knees,
Pray to the gods to intermit the plague
That needs must light on this ingratitude.

Murellus

1 Wherefore rejoyce?

2   What Conquest brings he home?

3 What Tributaries follow him to Rome,
   To grace in Captive bonds his Chariot Wheeles?

4 You Blockes, you stones, you worse [then] senslesse things:
   O you hard hearts, you cruell men of Rome,
   Knew you not Pompey many a time and oft?

5 Have you climb'd up to Walles and Battlements,
   To Towres and Windowes?

6   Yea, to Chimney tops,
  Your Infants in your Armes, and there have sate
   The live-long day, with patient expectation,
   To see great Pompey passe the streets of Rome :
   And when you saw his Chariot but appeare,
   Have you not made an Universall shout,
   That [Tyber] trembled underneath her bankes
   To heare the replication of your sounds,
   Made in her Concave Shores?

7 And do you now put on your best attyre?

8 And do you now cull out a Holyday?

9 And do you now strew Flowers in his way,
   That comes in Triumph over Pompeyes blood?

10 Be gone,
   Runne to your houses, fall upon your knees,
   Pray to the Gods to intermit the plague
   That needs must light on this Ingratitude .

• despite this, it seems that Murellus can contain his feelings, for the first three sentences of rebuke are highly factual (6/2)

• but as the insults intensify (comparing the crowd to 'worse than senslesse things' – one of the most appalling denigrations to Elizabethans who prided their sense of humanity above all things), so not only does the lack of grammar referred to above kick in, Murellus also becomes highly passionate (7/6 in just the four and a half lines of F #4-5)

• though he almost regains self-control in F #6's opening description of how the people used to sit in wait for their previous hero, Pompey, 'The live-long day, with patient expectation' (5/2, the first three and a half lines) Murellus' passions quickly take over once again at the memory how they received Pompey 'with 'an Universall shout' (5/4, F #6's remaining five lines)

• the ensuing three sentences as to how they now respond to Cæsar (F #7 putting on their 'best attyre', #8's calling it a 'Holiday', and #9's strewing 'Flowers in his way') are also passionate (4/3), the shortness of F #7-8 suggest that, as with the opening, Murellus ia once more almost at a loss for words

• fascinatingly, by the start of F #10's final instruction "Be gone,/Runne to your houses, fall upon your knees,' - with the two unembellished phrases surrounding the emotional command to 'Runne' - it seems his energy is almost dissipated, and the final interdiction to 'Pray' becomes bleakly intellectual (2/0, the last two lines of the speech)

The Tragedie of Julius Cæsar

Decius

This Dreame is all amisse interpreted,
between 2.2.83 - 104

Background: During the anti-Cæsar plotting the subject of Cæsar's basing his actions on prophecy was raised, fearing that, should the circumstances not seem favourable, Cæsar might not attend the Senate the day the assassination is planned. Decius then suggested that there was no need to worry, for Decius knows how to handle the problem should it arise. Here it has, and he does.

Style: as part of a three-handed scene

Where: Cæsar's home

To Whom: Cæsar and Calphurnia, and perhaps a servant

# of Lines: 22

Probable Timing: 1.10 minutes

Decius

1 This dream is all amiss interpreted,
   It was a vision fair and fortunate .

2 Your statue spouting blood in many pipes,
   In which so many smiling Romans bath'd,
   Signifies that from you great Rome shall suck
   Reviving blood, and that great men shall press
   For tinctures, stains, relics, and cognizance .

3 This by Calphurnia's dream is signified .

4 And { you shall say I have} well expounded it {,}
{†} When you have heard what I can say ;
   And know it now : the Senate have concluded
   To give this day a crown to mighty Cæsar .

5 If you shall send them word you will not come,
   Their minds may change .

6   Besides, it were a mock
   Apt to be render'd, for some one to say,
   "Break up the Senate till another time,
   When Cæsar's wife shall meet with better dreams."

7 If Cæsar hide himself, shall they not whisper,
   "Lo Cæsar is afraid?"

8 Pardon me, Cæsar, for my dear dear love
   To your proceeding bids me tell you this ;
   And reason to my love is liable .

Decius

1　This Dreame is all amisse interpreted,
　　It was a vision, faire and fortunate :
　　Your Statue spouting blood in many pipes,
　　In which so many smiling Romans bath'd,
　　Signifies, that from you great Rome shall sucke
　　Reviving blood, and that great men shall presse
　　For Tinctures, Staines, Reliques, and Cognisance .

2　This by Calphurnia's Dreame is signified.

3　And { you shall say I have} well expounded it {,}
{†}　When you have heard what I can say :
　　And know it now, the Senate have concluded
　　To give this day, a Crowne to mighty Cæsar .

4　If you shall send them word you will not come,
　　Their mindes may change .

5　　　　　　　　　　　　　Besides, it were a mocke
　　Apt to be render'd, for some one to say,
　　Breake up the Senate, till another time :
　　When Cæsars wife shall meete with better Dreames .

6　If Cæsar hide himselfe, shall they not whisper
　　Loe Cæsar is affraid?

7　Pardon me Cæsar, for my deere deere love
　　To your proceeding, bids me tell you this :
　　And reason to my love is liable .

- F #1's onrush suggests that there is far more urgency to interpret the 'Dreame' the way the conspirators wish for the F Decius than for his modern counterpart, especially since the first two lines open emotionally (1/3), and require the first of four extra breath-thoughts

- and though he continues onrushed, at the same time he begins to evince control, the reinterpretation that 'from you great Rome shall sucke/Reviving blood' becoming intellectual (9/5, F #1's last five lines and the short F #2)

- indeed F #3's unembellished tempting-tease of what he is about to say

  "And { you shall say I have} well expounded it {,}/{}when you have heard what I can say: /And know it now,"

  suggests that the easy calm of his seductive powers are now at their very best, with the follow up of announcement that

  "the Senate have concluded/To give this day a Crowne, to mighty Cæsar."

  being splendidly factual (3/1)

- and having shown his ability to stay calm, as Decius begins to ridicule Cæsar's possible refusal with what people will say, wait till 'Cæsar's wife shall meete with better Dreames' (heightened by being set as a surround phrase) or, worse, 'Loe Cæsar is affraid', he becomes passionately emotional (6/10, the seven lines F #4-6 and the first line of F #7) – though whether this is genuine or mere manipulation (of which he boasts he is a master, especially as far as Cæsar is concerned, in a previous scene with the conspirators) is up to each actor to decide

- certainly he is very careful in excusing himself from any possible insult to either Cæsar or Calphurnia, for after the emotional explanation that it is 'my deere deere love' the final

  "bids me tell you this : /And reason to my love is liable . "

  is unembellished, and ends with a determined surround phrase, only the second in the speech

The Tragedie of Hamlet, Prince of Denmarke

Hamlet

I will tell you why {you were sent for;} so shall my anticipation

2.2.293 - 310

Background: In stripping Rosincrance and Guildensterne of any
pretence of friendship and thus revealing them to be spies for
Claudius and Gertrude, Hamlet eventually does make an attempt
to explain his current disaffection (with the strange punctuation
of the First Folio revealing just how difficult it is for him to put
coherent thoughts together, at least for now).

Style: as part of a three-handed scene

Where: the lobby of the castle

To Whom: Rosincrance and Guildensterne

# of Lines: 18

Probable Timing: 0.55 minutes

Take Note: The hallmark of this speech as set in F is that Hamlet is
having difficulty in expressing himself, as evidenced by the punctuation and phrasing going awry - as if his feigned 'madness' has
led him almost to a momentary loss of reason: this pattern is re-
peated more and more, especially in F, until the meeting with Os-
ricke: as seen here, most modern texts tend to repunctuate for rationality, and in so doing probably lose one of the most important
character developments and struggles that Hamlet faces throughout the middle and later sequences of the play.

Hamlet

1   I will tell you why {you were sent for ;} so shall my anticipa-
    tion prevent your discovery, [and] your secrecy to the King
    and Queen moult no feather .

2   I have of late - but wherefore
    I know not - lost all my mirth, forgone all custom of ex-
    ercise; and indeed it goes so [heavily] with my dispositi-
    on, that this goodly frame, the earth, seems to me a ster-
    rile promontory; this most excellent canopy, the air,
    look you, this brave o'erhanging [firmament], this majest-
    ical roof fretted with golden fire, why, it [appeareth
    nothing] to me [but] a foul and pestilent congregation of
    vapors.

3   What a piece of work is a man, how noble in
    reason, how infinite in [faculties,] in form and moving,
    how express and admirable in action, how like an an-
    gel in apprehension, how like a god! the beauty of the
    world;   the paragon of animals; and yet to me what is
    this quintessence of dust?

4   Man delights not me - [ ]
    nor [women] neither, though by your smiling you seem
    to say so.

Hamlet

1 I will tell you why {you were sent for ;} so shall my anticipation prevent your discovery [of] your secricie to the King and
   Queene: moult no feather, I have of late, but wherefore
   I know not, lost all my mirth, forgone all custome of ex-
   ercise; and indeed, it goes so [heavenly] with my dispositi-
   on; that this goodly frame the Earth, seemes to me a ster-
   rill Promontory; this most excellent Canopy the Ayre,
   look you, this brave ore-hanging,[ ] this Majesticall Roofe,
   fretted with golden fire: why, it [appeares no other thing]
   to mee, [then] a foule and pestilent congregation of va-
   pours.

2   What a piece of worke is a man! how Noble in
   Reason? how infinite in [faculty?] in forme and moving
   how expresse and admirable? in Action, how like an Angel? in apprehension, how like a God? the beauty of the
   world, the Parragon of Animals; and yet to me, what is
   this Quintessence of Dust?

3   Man delights not me; [no],
   nor [Woman] neither; though by your smiling you seeme
   to say so.

• the enormously quiet opening is very unusual (the first five lines main-
ly unembellished, 2/2, save for the cluster of both capitals and one
long spelling referring to his uncle and mother by their formal titles
'King' and 'Queene') - a quiet which could suggest either a deliberately deceptive calm as he breaks to Rosincrance and Guildensterne his
knowledge of their spying on him, or a character desperately trying
to prevent himself from snapping under the strain of yet another act
of betrayal

• however, once he begins to explain how he regards 'this goodly frame
the Earth', first his passion breaks through in listing its supposed
beauty (6/5 the three and half lines to 'golden fire:') only to then fin-
ish emotionally as he describes its appearance to him as 'foule and
pestilent' (0/3, F #1's last two lines)

• while F #2's listing of the supposed beauty of man is deeply intellectual (9/3, F #2), its staggeringly ungrammatical punctuation and its
opening with six successive surround phrases point to a mind under-
going tremendous strain

• and though in terms of release F #3 seems to regain some control, the
three surround phrases formed by the two emotional semicolons underscore the strain beneath the extraordinarily bleak words

The Tragedie of Hamlet, Prince of Denmarke

Hamlet

I do not well understand that. Will you play/upon this Pipe?

between 3.2.250 - 373

Background: Following the confusion stemming from Claudius' abrupt closing down of 'The Murther of Gozago' Guildensterne has revealed himself to be much move closely allied with Claudius and Gertrude. He has delivered news of the 'King' being 'in his retyrement, marvellous distemper'd', and that the 'Queene ... hath sent me to you' since Hamlet's 'behavior hath stroke her into amazement'. Hamlet thus demands of Guildensterne an explanation of himself, to which Guildensterne has replied 'O my Lord, if my Dutie be too bold, my love is too unmannerly'. This response Hamlet promptly deflates - a musical instrument, a recorder, just having been brought into the room.

Style: one on one in front of a larger group

Where: wherever 'The Muder of Gonzago' has been played

To Whom: Guildensterne, in front of Rosincrance, Horatio, and some (or all) of the Players

# of Lines: 16

Probable Timing: 0.50 minutes

Take Note: F's orthography clearly shows how Hamlet's quiet self-control eventually disappears - whether as a deliberate ploy, or because he is genuinely angry at the treachery of his so-called friends, is up to each

Hamlet

1   I do not well understand that .

2   Will you play
upon this pipe ?

_____

3   I pray you .

_____

4   I do beseech you .

_____

5   'Tis as easy as lying .

6   Govern these ventages
with your finger and [thumbs], give it breath with your
mouth, and it will discourse most [eloquent] music .

7   Look you, these are the stops.

_____

8   Why, look you now, how unworthy a thing
you make of me !

9   You would play upon me, you would
seem to know my stops, you would pluck out the heart
of my mystery, you would sound me from my lowest
note to the top of my compass ; and there is much
music, excellent voice, in this little organ, yet cannot
you make it [speak] .

10   [S'blood] do you think, [ ] I am easier
to be play'd on, [than] a pipe ?

11   Call me what instrument you will,
though you can fret me, [yet] you cannot play upon me .

12   God
bless you, sir.

Hamlet

1   I do not well understand that.

2   Will you play
upon this Pipe?

3   I pray you.

4   I do beseech you.

5   'Tis as easie as lying: governe these Ventiges
with your finger and [thumbe], give it breath with your
mouth, and it will discourse most [excellent] Musicke.

6   Looke you, these are the stoppes.

7   Why looke you now, how unworthy a thing
you make of me: you would play upon mee; you would
seeme to know my stops: you would pluck out the heart
of my Mysterie;   you would sound mee from my lowest
Note, to the top of my Compasse: and there is much
Musicke, excellent Voice, in this little Organe, yet cannot
you make it [ ].

8   [Why] do you thinke, [that] I am easier
to bee plaid on, [then] a Pipe?

9   Call me what Instrument you will,
though you can fret me, [ ] you cannot play upon me.

10   God
blesse you Sir.

• Hamlet opens his challenge to Claudius' spies deceptively quietly (1/0, the first four short sentences - in themselves sufficient warning to his listeners that something is very wrong), and the opening unembellished surround phrase of F #5, the naked attack of ' . 'Tis as easie as lying ; '

• then, having essentially accused Rosincrance and Guildensterne of 'lying', his emotions break through as he goes through the motions of explaining to them how to play the recorder (2/4, the remainder of F #5)

• now that the emotions have broken through, they continue (0/3, F #7's first two and half lines) as he becomes even more direct in his attack, starting the 'how unworthy a thing you make of me' passage with five consecutive surround phrases, the last four of which are heightened by being linked in part by the emotional semicolons

> " . Why looke you now, how unworthy a thing you make of me: you
>
> would play upon mee ; you would seeme to know my stops :
>
> you would pluck out the heart of my Mysterie ; you would
>
> sound mee from my lowest Note, to the top of my Compasse : "

• then his scorn? anger? turns to passion as he lays into them for their desire to 'pluck out the heart of my Mysterie' (6/4, the last four lines of F #7)

• and as the speech ends, the passion intensifies as Hamlet finally demands an answer from them (F #8-9) and then challenges the entry of Polonius (3/2, F #8-10) in that these last three sentences are all short and directly to the point

The Tragedie of Hamlet, Prince of Denmarke
Clown

Is she to bee buried in Christian buriall,
between 5.1.1 - 29

Background: Despite the suspicion that Ophelia committed suicide and therefore should not be accorded a Christian burial (see the following speech), she is to be buried in sanctified ground, to the surprise of the Gravediggers.

Style: as part of a two-handed scene

Where: a grave-yard

To Whom: his fellow Grave-Digger/Clowne

# of Lines: 19

Probable Timing: 1.00 minutes

Take Note: It seems that the Clown becomes very emotional when debating (whether this particular situation is pleasurable or the class-struggle unfairness of an upper class suicide being allowed a Christian burial has riled him is up to each actor to explore), for in the long sequence of sixteen consecutive surround phrases (F #3-6) suggesting that he is pushing his argument quite relentlessly, no fewer than eight of the twelve pieces of major punctuation are emotional semicolons.

Clown

1   Is she to be buried in Christian burial [when she]
     willfully seeks her own salvation?

2   How can that be, unless she drowned herself in
     her own defense?

3   It must be se offendendo, it cannot be else.
4   For here
     lies the point: if I drown myself wittingly, it ar-
     gues an act, and an act hath three branches - it is [to]
     act, to do, and to perform; argal, she drown'd herself
     wittingly.

5   Give me leave.
6   Here lies the water; good.
7   Here stands the man; good.
8   If the man go to this wa-
     ter and drown himself, it is, will he, nill he, he goes,
     mark you that?
9   But if the water come to him & drown
     him, he drowns not himself; argal, he that is
     not guilty of his own death shortens not his own life.

10   Will you ha' the truth on't.
11   If this had not
     been a gentlewoman, she should have been buried
     out ['a] Christian burial.

12   {† T}he more pity that
     great folk should have count'nance in this world to
     drown or hang themselves, more [than] their even Christi-
     an .

Clown

1   Is she to bee buried in Christian buriall, [that]
    wilfully seekes her owne salvation ?

---

2   How can that be, unlesse she drowned her selfe in
    her owne defence?

---

3   It must be *Se offendendo*, it cannot bee else :   for heere
    lies the point;   If I drowne my selfe wittingly, it ar-
    gues an Act: and an Act hath three branches.

4   It is [an] Act
    to doe and to performe;   argall she drown'd her selfe
    wittingly.

---

5   Give me leave;   heere lies the water;   good:
    heere stands the man;   good: If the man goe to this wa-
    ter and drowne himselfe;   it is will he nill he, he goes;
    marke you that?

6   But if the water come to him & drowne
    him;   hee drownes not himselfe.

7   Argall, hee that is
    not guilty of his owne death, shortens not his owne life.

---

8   Will you ha the truth on't: If this had not
    beene a Gentlewoman, shee should have beene buried
    out [of] Christian Buriall.

---

9   {† T}he more pitty that
    great folke should have countenance in this world to
    drowne or hang themselves, more [then] their even Christi-
    an .

- in questioning the idea of 'Christian buriall' even before the intense debate manifests itself, the speech starts emotionally (1/7, F #1-2)

- the moment the assertion that it was suicide ('Se offendendo') is spoken aloud, the Clowne becomes passionate (4/4, F #3), but the heightened surround phrase elaboration as to why it must be considered suicide (F #5-7) turns very emotional (1/14)

- after the proof is finished comes a very careful monosyllabic unembellished surround phrase ' . Will you ha the truth on't : ' (perhaps pointing to the underlying political awareness beneath the Clowne's more usually accepted mask of fun and humour), which springs into a second passionate release (4/4, F #8's remaining two lines) as the key social class distinction is voiced

- which in turn leads to a final emotional class struggle denunciation of the privileges 'great folke' seem to have when compared to other Christians (0/4, F #9)

The Tragedie of Hamlet, Prince of Denmarke

Priest

Her Obsequies have bin as farre inlarg'd,
between 5.1.226 - 238

Background: At the King's command, Ophelia is being buried in holy ground. The event is being handled before a tiny group of mourners with as little ceremony as possible, offending her brother mightily, who has demanded twice 'What Cerimony else?'. The following is the Priest's unequivocal reply.

Style: initially to one man, for the benefit of the small group present

Where: a grave-yard

To Whom: Laertes, in front of the King and Queene, some 'Lords attendant', with Hamlet and Horatio watching unobserved

# of Lines: 12

Probable Timing: 0.40 minutes

Take Note: F's orthography points not only to just how disturbed the priest is, but also where he gains and loses self-control.

Priest

1   Her obsequies have been as far enlarg'd
     As we have [warranty].

2   Her death was doubtful,
     And but that great command, o'ersways the order,
     She should in ground unsanctified [been] lodg'd
     Till the last trumpet ; for charitable [prayers],
     Shards, flints, and pebbles should be thrown on her .

3   Yet here she is allowed her virgin [crants],
     Her maiden strewments, and the bringing home
     Of bell and burial .

----

5   {To do more }
     We should profane the service of the dead
     To sing [a] requiem and such rest to her
     As to peace-parted souls.

Priest

1   Her Obsequies have bin as farre inlarg'd,
    As we have [warrantis], her death was doubtfull,
    And but that great Command, o're-swaies the order,
    She should in ground unsanctified [have] lodg'd,
    Till the last Trumpet .

2   For charitable [praier],
    Shardes, Flints, and Peebles, should be throwne on her :
    Yet heere she is allowed her Virgin [Rites],
    Her Maiden strewments, and the bringing home
    Of Bell and Buriall .

   _____

3   {To do more }
    We should prophane the service of the dead,
    To sing [sage] Requiem, and such rest to her
    As to peace-parted Soules .

- his outlining of the facts of what has occurred so far, including political interference, starts passionately (3/2, F #1)

- and the Priest becomes even more passionate in the explanation of what really should be the treatment for Ophelia, as for any suicide, (2/3 in F #2's first line and a half)

    " . For charitable [praier],/Shardes, Flints, and Peebles, should be throwne on her: "

- and then he seems to gain a good degree of self-control as he explains what rights have been granted her thanks to political interference (5/2, the remainder of F #2)

- but then in his protest that to do even more would 'prophane the service of the dead' it seems that self-control begins to crack, for this final sentence is passionate – though not overly so (2/2), perhaps suggesting that he is being quite circumspect in this protest (attempting to save his own skin)

The Tragedie of Troylus and Cressida
Thersites

A wonder. /Ajax goes up and downe the field, asking for
between 3.3.242 - 265

Background: as found in Homer's *Iliad* this very bitter character
was accounted an officer, and eventually killed by Achilles who,
like everyone else, grew tired of his attacks: here, in the following
three speeches, is Shakespeare's version heard in all his insulting
and wondrously foul-mouthed glory. In this speech Thersites
brings news to Achilles that the generals have selected Ajax and
not Achilles for the following day's honour of single combat with
the Trojan Hector

Style: three-handed scene

Where: in the Greek camp

To Whom: Achilles in front of Patroclus;

# of Lines: 20

Probable Timing: 1.00 minutes

Take Note: Compared to his much more intellect-emotion balanced
face to face quarrel with Patroclus in the following speech (16/15
overall), here, in his audience- direct mocking of Ajax, Thersites
is very emotional (9/28).

Thersites

1   A wonder !

---

2   Ajax goes up and down the field, asking for
    himself .

---

3   He must fight singly to-morrow with Hector,
    and is so prophetically proud of an heroical cudgelling
    that he raves in saying nothing .

---

4   Why, [a] stalks up and down like a peacock - a
    stride and a stand ; ruminates like an hostess that hath
    no arithmetic but her brain to set down her recko-
    ning ; bites his lip with a politic regard, as who should
    say, "There were wit in [this] head and 'twould out" - and
    so there is ; but it lies as coldly in him as fire in a flint,
    which will not show without knocking .

5   The man's undone
    for ever, for if Hector break not his neck i'th'com-
    bat, he'll break't himself in vainglory .

6   He knows
    not me .

7   I said, "Good morrow Ajax" ;   and he replies,
    "Thanks Agamemnon ."

8   What think you of this man
    that takes me for the general ?

9   He's grown a very
    land-fish, languageless, a monster .

10   A plague of o-
    pinion ! a man may wear it on both sides, like a leather
    jerkin .

Thersites

1 A wonder.

2 Ajax goes up and downe the field, asking for
   himselfe .

3 Hee must fight singly to morrow with Hector,
   and is so prophetically proud of an heroicall cudgelling,
   that he raves in saying nothing .

4 Why he stalkes up and downe like a Peacock, a
   stride and a stand : ruminates like an hostesse, that hath
   no Arithmatique but her braine to set downe her recko-
   ning : bites his lip with a politique regard, as who should
   say, there were wit in [his] head and twoo'd out ; and
   so there is : but it lyes as coldly in him, as fire in a flint,
   which will not shew without knocking .

5   The mans undone
   for ever ; for if Hector breake not his necke i'th'combat, heele break't himselfe in vaine-glory .

6   He knowes
   not mee : I said, good morrow Ajax ; And he replyes,
   thankes Agamemnon .

7   What thinke you of this man,
   that takes me for the Generall ?

8   Hee's growne a very
   land-fish, languagelesse, a monster : a plague of o-
   pinion, a man may weare it on both sides like a leather
   Jerkin .

- Thersites starts deceptively quietly, though the shortness of the unembellished F #1 should suggest something is about to break –

- - and it does, but slowly, for while F #2-3's start to the put down of Ajax, simply setting up the facts of Ajax talking to himself in public, is mildly emotional (1/4 in four lines), the extended F #4's wonderfully wicked descriptions of Ajax's 'Peacock/hostesse'-like behaviour suddenly explodes emotionally (2/9 in six and a half lines), reinforced by three surround phrases, two of them formed in part by an (emotional) semicolon

- and following Thersites' unembellished surround phrase suggestion 'The mans undone for ever ; ' (again deceptively quiet, calm in his own certainty perhaps) the idea of Ajax's neck being broken either by his opponent Hector or by Ajax's owne 'vaine-glory' allows his emotion to sweep in once more (1/5 in just over one line)

- the fact that in his bemusement Ajax mistook Thersites for the general Agamemnon is spoken of with (delighted?) passion (F #6, 3/4), enhanced by F #6 being set as three surround phrases (two of which are emotional)

  " , He knowes not mee : I said, good morrow Ajax ; And he replyes,

    thankes Agamemnon. "

- and Thersites' emotion continues to be released with his final questioning the audience as to 'What thinke you of this man, . . . ', as well as the final summation, again starting with the surround phrase heightening Thersites' own assessment of Ajax ' . Hee's growne a very land-fish, languagelesse, a monster : ' (2/6, F #7-8)

The Tragedie of Troylus and Cressida

Thersites

Prythee be silent boy, I profit not by thy talke,
between 5.1.14 - 36

Background: In this speech Thersites pulls no punches as he names
Patroclus to his face as Achilles' male whore

Style: three-handed scene;

Where: the Greek camp

To Whom: Patroclus in front of Achilles;

# of Lines: 11

Probable Timing: 0.40 minutes

Take Note: Compared to his audience- direct mocking of Ajax,
where Thersites was very emotional (9/28, speech #13 above),
here in his face to face quarrel with Patroclus, he is much more
passionate s (16/15 overall), the bracketed and shaded Q only
text, usually set by most modern texts, adding to the list of
horrors and insults piled upon 'Achilles male Varlot'.

Thersites

1   Prythee be silent, boy, I profit not by thy talk .

2   Thou art [said] to be Achilles' male varlot{, }

────────

his masculine whore .

3   Now the rotten diseases
of the south, [the] guts-griping, ruptures, catarrhs,
loads of a gravel i'th'back, lethargies, cold palsies, [raw
eyes, dirt rotten livers, [wheezing] lungs, bladders
full of imposthurne, sciaticas lime-kills ith'palme,
incurable bone-ache, and the rivell'd fee simple of the
tetter] take and take again such preposterous discove-
ries !

────────────────

4   {†}   {T}hou idle
immaterial skein of [sleave]- silk ; thou green sarcenet
flap for a sore eye, thou tassle of a prodigal's purse, thou {.}

5   Ah, how the poore world is pest'red with such water-flies,
diminutives of nature !

────────

6   Finch-egg !

Thersites

1 Prythee be silent boy, I profit not by thy talke,
   thou art [thought] to be Achilles male Varlot{, }

   ---

   his masculine Whore.

2   Now the rotten diseases
   of the South, [ ] guts-griping Ruptures, Catarres,
   Loades of a gravell i'th'backe, Lethargies, cold Palsies, [and
   the like], take and take againe, such prepostrous discove-
   ries .

   ---

3 {†}   {T}hou idle,
   immateriall skiene of [Sleyd] silke ; thou greene Sarcenet
   flap for a sore eye, thou tassell of a Prodigals purse thou :
   Ah how the poore world is pestred with such water-flies,
   diminutives of Nature .

   ---

4 Finch Egge.

- the speech remains passionate almost throughout, with intellect slightly dominating emotion in F #1, #2 and #4

- however, once the insults of F #3 based on images of slightness and vanity begin ('Sley'd silke' – or 'sleave' silk as most modern would have it – being a form of silk that can be broken down into smaller components, and 'Sarcenet' being an inferior form of silk used for linings rather than show in the best of clothing), not only does emotion dominate for a moment (3/6, the first two and half lines), the power of both the opening of the insult

" . Thou idle, immateriall skiene of [Sleyd] silke ;"

and the sentence ending summation

" . Ah how the poore world is pestred with such water-flies,

    diminutives of Nature."

are intensified by being set as the only surround phrases in the speech, the first even further heightened by being formed in part by the only emotional semicolon of the piece

The Tragedie of Troylus and Cressida

Thersites

With too much bloud, and too little Brain, these

5.1.48 - 66

Background: Alone, Thersites sums up the whole Greek command

Style: solo

Where: in the Greek camp

To Whom: direct audience address

# of Lines: 18

Probable Timing: 0.55 minutes

Take Note: Thersites' contempt knows neither bounds nor rank, for after dismissing both Achilles and Patroclus (F #1) he then goes on to insult two of the Princes, and while at least his passionate (3/4) contempt for the General Agamemnon is somewhat tempered by grudging respect, the all-over-the-place pulling apart of Agamemnon's brother Menelaus (over whose wayward wife the war is being fought) shows no such respect.

Thersites

1   With too much blood, and too little brain, these
     two may run mad, but, if with too much brain and too
     little blood they do, I'll be a curer of madmen .

2   Here's
     Agamemnon, an honest fellow enough, and one that loves
     quails, but he has not so much brain as ear-wax ; and
     the goodly transformation of Jupiter there, his brother,
     the bull, the primitive statue and oblique memorial of
     cuckolds, a thrifty shoeing-horn in a chain, [ ]
     at his brother's leg - to what [form] but that he is, should
     wit larded with malice, and malice forced with wit, turn
     him to ?

3   To an ass, were nothing, he is both ass and
     ox ; to an ox, were nothing, he is both ox and ass .

4   To be a dog, a mule, a cat, a [fitchook], a toad, a li-
     zard, an owl, a puttock, or a herring without a roe,
     I would not care ; but to be Menelaus, I would conspire
     against destiny .

5   Ask me not what I would be if I were
     not Thersites, for I care not to be the louse of a lazar,
     so I were not Menelaus .

Thersites

1　With too much bloud, and too little Brain, these
two may run mad : but if with too much braine, and too
little blood, they do, Ile be a curer of madmen .

2　　　　　　　　　　　　　　　　　Heere's
Agamemnon, an honest fellow enough, and one that loves
Quailes, but he has not so much Braine as eare-wa ; and
the goodly transformation of Jupiter there his Brother,
the Bull, the primative Statue, and oblique memoriall of
Cuckolds, a thrifty shooing-horne in a chaine, [hanging]
at his Brothers legge, to what for me but that he is, shold
wit larded with malice, and malice forced with wit, turne
him too : to an Asse were nothing ; hee is both Asse and
Oxe ; to an Oxe were nothing, hee is both Oxe and Asse :
to be a Dogge ; a Mule, a Cat, a [Fitchew], a Toade, a Li-
zard, an Owle, a Puttocke, or a Herring without a Roe,
I would not care : but to be Menelaus, I would conspire
against Destiny .

3　　　　　　　　　　　　Aske me not what I would be, if I were
not Thersites : for I care not to bee the lowse of a Lazar,
so I were not Menelaus .

- though starting with a surround phrase, Thersites' F #1 dismissal of Achilles and Patroclus as being essentially brainless is an easy (resigned?) mixture of intellect, emotion (1/2) and unembellishment

- F #2's opening two line passionate dismissal of Agamemnon is much more energetic (3/4), and then the first two line extension to Agammemnon's brother, the start of what turns into a lengthy diatribe (dismissing him as a 'primative Statue'), opens intellectually (4/0)

- and then in expanding the contempt to (correctly) describe Menelaus as a Cuckold getting his status from the power of his brother, Thersites' emotions get the better of him (2/7, the next three and a half lines)

- F #2 ends with the intellectual surround phrase ' : but to be Menelaus, I would conspire against Destiny . ' (2/0), the build up to this first of two unequivocal conclusions, listing anything Thersites would rather be is amazingly passionate (16/12 in just four lines, including four surround phrases)

- F #3's summation, essentially an even more vehement restatement of the end of F #2 is equally passionate (3/3), its passion extra weighted by being set as two surround phrases

The Tragedie of Othello, The Moore of Venice

Iago

O Sir content you. /I follow him, to serve my turne upon him.

1.1.41 - 65

Background: Iago has been handsomely paid by Rodorigo to woo
Desdemona on Rodorigo's behalf, unsuccessfully as it turns out,
since she has just secretly married Othello, Iagos' military supe-
rior: unknown to Rodorigo, Iago has been pocketing Rodorigo's
gifts (money and jewels) to Desdemona, and in order to keep the
bounty flowing it's essential for Iago to prove to Rodorigo that he
hates Othello (not a difficult task, for he really does): this speech
allows Iago to expand on his personal philosophy

Style: as part of a two-handed scene

Where: a street near the home of Desdemona's father

To Whom: Rodorigo

# of Lines: 27

Probable Timing: 1.30 minutes

Take Note: The passion that ended his last speech infuses this
speech throughout (17/23 overall), with F's orthography suggesting some very interesting cracks in Iago's self-control.

Iago

1   O, sir, content you ;
     I follow him to serve my turn upon him.

2   We cannot be [all] masters, nor all masters
     Cannot be truly follow'd.

3   You shall mark
     Many a duteous and knee-crooking knave
     That (doting on his own obsequious bondage)
     Wears out his time, much like his master's ass,
     For naught but provender, & when he's old , cashier'd.

4   Whip me such honest knaves.

5   Others there are
     Who, trimm'd in forms and visages of duty,
     Keep yet their hearts attending on themselves,
     And throwing but shows of service on their lords,
     Do well thrive by them; and when they have lin'd their
                                                    coats,
     Do themselves homage .

6   [Those] fellows have some soul,
     And such a one do I profess myself.

7   For, sir,
     It is as sure as you are Rodorigo,
     Were I the Moor, I would not be Iago.

8   In following him, I follow but myself;
     Heaven is my judge, not I for love and duty,
     But seeming so, for my peculiar end;
     For when my outward action doth demonstrate
     The native act, and figure of my heart
     In complement extern, 'tis not long after
     But I will wear my heart upon my sleeve
     For [Doves] to peck at: I am not what I am.

Iago

1   O Sir content you.

2   I follow him, to serve my turne upon him.

3   We cannot [all be] Masters, nor all Masters
     Cannot be truely follow'd.

4   You shall marke
     Many a dutious and knee-crooking knave;
     That (doting on his owne obsequious bondage)
     Weares out his time, much like his Masters Asse,
     For naught but Provender, & when he's old Casheer'd.

5   Whip me such honest knaves.

6   Others there are
     Who trym'd in Formes, and visages of Dutie,
     Keepe yet their hearts attending on themselves,
     And throwing but showes of Service on their Lords
     Doe well thrive by them.

7   And when they have lin'd their Coates
     Doe themselves Homage.

8   [These] Fellowes have some soule,
     And such a one do I professe my selfe.

9   For (Sir)
     It is as sure as you are Rodorigo,
     Were I the Moore, I would not be Iago:
     In following him, I follow but my selfe.

10   Heaven is my Judge, not I for love and dutie,
     But seeming so, for my peculiar end:
     For when my outward Action doth demonstrate
     The native act, and figure of my heart
     In Complement externe, 'tis not long after
     But I will weare my heart upon my sleeve
     For [Dawes] to pecke at ; I am not what I am .

• the whole tenor of the speech seems to stem from F #5's one unembellished short sentence as Iago, having described any honest servant as a 'knee-crooking knave', the equivalent of their 'Masters Asse', finally dismisses them with

" Whip me such honest knaves."

• and this is counterbalanced/expanded by the only logical surround phrase in the speech, that in serving Othello Iago is in fact putting his own interests above all, explaining that

" : In following him, I follow but my selfe . "

• that this conviction is so deep set it knocks him off balance can be seen as he describes himself as his own self-serving master, so F #7-8 set four short lines (five/six/five/six syllables)

• it's also possible that the small pauses therein not only indicate Iago is taking great care to exert self-control as he explains his philosophy very precisely, they might show he is pausing just to see how Rodorigo is reacting to such an out and out statement of practiced deceit

• interestingly, the lead into this is via the first of only two emotional surround phrases, F #4's

" . You shall marke/Many a dutious and knee-crooking knave ; "

• the two emotional moments underscore

a/ Iago's metrical irregular admiration of 'These Fellowes' (F #8, 1/4)
b/ the final lead up to the second emotional surround phrase of self definition, ' ; I am not what I am .", its enormity heightened by being both monosyllabic and unembellished too

• and, in what must be remembered throughout the rest of the play, the only intellectual moment in the speech marks the moment when Iago swears that 'Heaven is my Judge' that all he does is not 'for love and dutie' but for 'my peculiar end' (3/1, F #10's first three and half lines)

The Tragedie of Othello, The Moore of Venice

Brabantio

Oh thou foule Theefe, / Where hast thou stow'd my Daughter ?

1.2.62 - 81

Background: Othello, an older man of colour (a 'Moore'), and a for-
eigner, is one of Venice's leading (mercenary) generals: he has secretly married young Desdemona, the only daughter of Brabantio,
a leading white Senator. Brabantio and his followers encounter
Othello and his men in the street on their way to the Senate

Style: one on one in front of a larger group for all to hear

Where: in a street in Venice

To Whom: Othello, in front of Othello's men including Cassio and
Iago, and Rodorigo plus members of Brabantio's household

# of Lines: 20

Probable Timing: 1.00 minutes

Brabantio

1   O thou foul thief, where hast thou stow'd my daughter ?

2   Damn'd as thou art, thou hast enchanted her,
For I'll refer me to all things of sense,
If she in chains of magic were not bound,
Whether a maid so tender, fair, and happy,
So opposite to marriage, that she shunn'd
The wealthy curled [darlings] of our nation,
Would ever have, t'encur a general mock,
Run from her guardage to the sooty bosom
Of such a thing as thou - to fear, not to delight !

3   Judge me the world, if 'tis not gross in sense,
That thou hast practic'd on her with foul charms,
Abus'd her delicate youth with drugs or minerals
That weakens motion .

4   I'll have't disputed on,
'Tis probable, and palpable to thinking .

5   I therefore apprehend and do attach thee
For an abuser of the world, a practicer
Of arts inhibited, and out of warrant .

6   Lay hold upon him, if he do resist
Subdue him, at his peril .

Brabantio

1   Oh thou foule Theefe,*
    Where hast thou stow'd my Daughter ?

2   Damn'd as thou art, thou hast enchaunted her
    For Ile referre me to all things of sense,
    (If she in Chaines of Magick were not bound)
    Whether a Maid, so tender, Faire, and Happie,
    So opposite to Marriage, that she shun'd
    The wealthy curled [Deareling] of our Nation,
    Would ever have (t'encurre a generall mocke)
    Run from her Guardage to the sootie bosome,
    Of such a thing as thou : to feare, not to delight ?

3   Judge me the world, if 'tis not grosse in sense,
    That thou hast practis'd on her with foule Charmes,
    Abus'd her delicate Youth, with Drugs or Minerals,
    That weakens Motion .

4   Ile have't disputed on,
    'Tis probable, and palpable to thinking ;
    I therefore apprehend and do attach thee,
    For an abuser of the World, a practiser
    Of Arts inhibited, and out of warrant ;
    Lay hold upon him, if he do resist
    Subdue him, at his perill .

• the opening split line gives Brabantio a moment to gather himself together before starting F #1's passionate attack on Othello (2/2), and as with Iago above, the key words in this first sentence are capitalised at line's end

• having made his meaning abundantly clear, Brabantio is equally passionate in accusing Othello of ensnaring Desdemona in 'Chaines of Magick', (8/6, F #2's first six lines) at least initially, but then in finishing the sentence with an out and out racial smear Brabantio's emotions come to the fore (1/5, F #2's last three lines) – perhaps giving himself away in his attitude towards race-relations with the first surround phrase in the speech, in suggesting that without 'Magick' Desdemona's response to Othello would have been ' : to feare, not to delight ? '

• and this emotion continues as Brabantio repeats the charge that Othello has 'practis'd on her with foule Charmes' (F #3's first two lines, 1/3), but then becoming factually driven as he elaborates the charges, suggesting that Othello used, 'Drugs or Minerals' (4/0, F #3's last two lines)

• and then despite Brabantio's attempts to rein himself in and recover some semblance of public dignity, and despite the two and a half unembellished lines deciding to take the matter to a judicial hearing ('Ile have't disputed on'), the cost of maintaining such public calm is enormous, for

  a/ unlike most modern texts which split the final passage into three separate sentences, F sets a single onrush jamming together the notion of judicial action, the arrest, and the command to his own forces to lay hold of Othello

  b/ the emotional semicolons only now make their appearance in this onrushed F #4, suggesting even the unembellished surround phrase idea of 'Ile have't disputed on,/'Tis probable, and palpable to thinking ; ' is not as calm as might first appear

• thus F #3's relative lack of release (0/0 for the idea of a hearing; 2/0 for the formal arrest; 0/1 for the 'Lay hold upon him . . . at his perill.' suggests an enforced calm struggling to control emotion rather than relaxed or easy self-control

The Tragedie of Macbeth

Old Man

Threescore and ten I can remember well,
between 3.1.1 - 19

Background: As the old man reports, since Duncan's death more supernatural events have occurred, matching those spoken of by Lenox. This speech is made up from lines originally assigned both to the Old Man and to Rosse.

Style: as part of a two-handed scene

Where: unspecified, but possibly somewhere on a public road

To Whom: Rosse

# of Lines: 20

Probable Timing: 1.00 minutes

Take Note: Throughout, the inner cracks in F's orthography point to just how much the strangeness of the 'Night' is affecting the Old man's recounting of events – each by themselves (the minor onrush of F #2-3, the information contained within the few surround phrases, the F only split line starting F #4, and the unembellished final horrific sentence) could be almost ignored, but when the upheaval in this seventy-odd year old's world is clearly visible put together.

Old Man

1 Threescore and ten I can remember well,
   Within the volume of which time I have seen
   Hours dreadful, and things strange ; but this sore night
   Hath trifled former knowing .

---

2 {†} Thou seest the heavens, as troubled with man's act,
   Threatens his bloody stage .
3   By th'clock 'tis day,
   And yet dark night strangles the [travelling] lamp .
4 Is't night's predominance, or the day's shame,
   That darkness does the face of earth entomb,
   When living light should kiss it ?

---

5   'Tis unnatural,
   Even like the deed that's done .
6   On Tuesday last,
   A falcon, tow'ring in her pride of place,
   Was by a mousing owl hawk'd at, and kill'd .

---

7 {†} And Duncan's horses (a thing most strange, and certain)
   Beauteous and swift, the minions of their race,
   Turn'd wild in nature, broke their stalls, flung out,
   Contending 'gainst obedience, as they would make
   War with mankind .

---

8   {T}hey {ate} each other,

{†} To th'amazement of mine eyes that look'd upon't.

Old Man

1   Threescore and ten I can remember well,
     Within the Volume of which Time, I have seene
     Houres dreadfull, and things strange : but this sore Night
     Hath trifled former knowings .

2{†} Thou seest the Heavens, as troubled with mans Act,
      Threatens his bloody Stage : by th'Clock 'tis Day,
      And yet darke Night strangles the [travailing] Lampe :
      Is't Nights predominance, or the Dayes shame,
      That Darknesse does the face of Earth intombe,
      When living Light should kisse it ?

---

3   'Tis unnaturall,
     Even like the deed that's done : On Tuesday last,
     A Faulcon towring in her pride of place,
     Was by a Mowsing Owle hawkt at, and kill'd .

4{†} And Duncans Horses,
      (A thing most strange, and certaine)
      Beauteous, and swift, the Minions of their Race,
      Turn'd wilde in nature, broke their stalls, flong out,
      Contending 'gainst Obedience, as they would
      Make Warre with Mankinde .

---

5   {T}hey {ate} each other,

{†} To th'amazement of mine eyes that look'd upon't.

• the surround phrases of F #1-3 point to the unnaturalness of what has occurred,

> " : but this sore Night/Hath trifled former knowings . /Thou seest the Heavens, as troubled with mans Act,/Threatens his bloody Stage : by th'Clock 'tis Day,/And yet darke Night strangles the [travailing] Lampe :"

> " . 'Tis unnaturall, Even like the deed that's done : "

and the onrush of the sentences, F #2's darkness at noon and F #3's first example of the overturning of the laws of nature, cause him so much disturbance that he waivers in his grammatical niceties (this clue is wiped out by most modern texts that divide them into three and two sentences respectively)

• and F #4's second example of overturned nature – Duncan's horses 'Contending 'gainst Obedience' - seem equally disturbing, for not only does the Old Man use two extra breath-thoughts to ensure that all of the details are heard, he also needs two short lines (five/seven syllables) to start – though most modern texts join the two together to create one longer twelve syllable line as shown

• the Old man opens passionately in declaring that this is the worst night he has experienced in his seventy years, (F #1, 3/3), he becomes strongly intellectual pointing to the 'Heavens . . troubled' as the cause (5/0, F #2's first two lines)

• but then passion takes over as he describes how the 'darke Night strangles' daylight (7/7, the four and half lines ending F #2 and the first line of F #3)

• in offering confirmation of the unnatural events, he becomes much more factual – though accompanied by some emotion – for both examples of animal revolt (the killing of the falcon and the disobedience of Duncan's horses) are intellectually handled (12/7)

• yet the final horror, of Duncan's horses eating each other, seems to strike the Old Man almost dumb, for F #5 is totally unembellished

The Tragedie of Macbeth

Lenox

My former Speeches,/Have but hit your Thoughts
3.6.1 - 24

Background: With the unusual number of deaths of people close to or standing in Macbeth's way, and especially after his most peculiar behaviour at the celebratory feast (where, in facing down the supposed ghost of Banquo - which only Macbeth could see - Macbeth opened a great deal of conjecture about his complicity in Banquo's death), people are beginning to talk, as here.

Style: as part of a two-handed scene

Where: unspecified, but perhaps close to the palace at Scone

To Whom: an un-named Lord

# of Lines: 24

Probable Timing: 1.15 minutes

Take Note: This is one of the finest oblique double-speak speeches in Shakespeare, for while Lenox ensures that his words cannot be used against him should any of Macbeth's spies overhear, nevertheless his language and phrasing probes much of Macbeth's actions to date – demanding that his listener commit himself one way or another before he does so himself – and F's orthography shows just how very careful and clever he can be.

Lenox

1   My former speeches have but hit your thoughts,
     Which can interpret farther ; only I say
     Things have been strangely born.

2   The gracious Duncan
     Was pitied of Macbeth ; marry, he was dead .

3   And the right valiant Banquo walk'd too late,
     Whom you may say (if't please you) [Fleance] kill'd,
     For [Fleance] fled .

4   Men must not walk too late .

5   Who cannot want the thought, how monstrous
     It was for Malcolm and for [Donalbain]
     To kill their gracious father ?

6   Damned fact !,

7   How it did grieve Macbeth !

8   Did he not straight
     In pious rage the two delinquents tear,
     That were the slaves of drink and thralls of sleep ?

9   Was not that nobly done ?

10   [Ay], and wisely too ;
     For 'twould have anger'd any heart alive
     To hear the men deny't .

11   So that, I say,
     He has borne all things well, and I do think
     That had he Duncan's sons under his key
     (As, and't please heaven he shall not) they should find
     What 'twere to kill a father ; so should [Fleance] .

12   But peace ! for from broad words, and 'cause he fail'd
     His presence at the tyrant's feast, I hear
     Macduff lives in disgrace .

13   Sir, can you tell
     Where he bestows himself ?

Lenox

1 My former Speeches
   Have but hit your Thoughts
   Which can interpret farther : Onely I say
   Things have bin strangely borne .

2   The gracious Duncan
   Was pittied of Macbeth : marry he was dead :
   And the right valiant Banquo walk'd too late,
   Whom you may say (if't please you) [Fleans] kill'd,
   For [Fleans] fled : Men must not walke too late .

3 Who cannot want the thought, how monstrous
   It was for Malcolme, and for [Donalbane]
   To kill their gracious Father ?

4   Damned Fact,
   How it did greeve Macbeth ?

5   Did he not straight
   In pious rage, the two delinquents teare,
   That were the Slaves of drinke, and thralles of sleepe ?

6 Was not that Nobly done ?

7   [I], and wisely too :
   For 'twould have anger'd any heart alive
   To heare the men deny't .

8   So that I say,
   He ha's borne all things well, and I do thinke,
   That had he Duncans Sonnes under his Key,
   (As, and't please Heaven he shall not) they should finde
   What 'twere to kill a Father : So should [Fleans] .

9 But peace ; for from broad words, and cause he fayl'd
   His presence at the Tyrants Feast, I heare
   Macduffe lives in disgrace .

10   Sir, can you tell
   Where he bestowes himselfe ?

- F's short opening lines (5/5 syllables) allow Lenox a very careful start as he embarks on what could be interpreted as treasonous remarks: most modern texts set them as one full line of verse, as shown, removing the opening clue

- his determined care is also seen both his intellectual control as he starts by posing the facts in a rather provocative way F #1-2 (9/4), and in the four surround phrases by which the key points are made

  " : Onely I say/Things have bin strangely borne . The gracious Duncan

     /Was pittied of Macbeth : marry he was dead : "

  " : Men must not walke too late . "

- Lenox then becomes passionate in raising F #3's more dangerous question of the involvement of Duncan's sons in their father's murder (3/2) and in F #4's even more dangerous notion of attaching Macbeth's grief to the event (2/1)

- then intellectual control almost completely disappears as he describes Macbeth's tearing apart of Duncan's supposed murderers and suggests that it was wisely done (2/5, F #5-7), the irony of the wording heightened by being expressed as two surround phrases

  " . I, and wisely too : /For 'twould have anger'd any heart alive/To heare the

     men deny't . "

- as Lenox so cleverly at one and the same time raises doubts about Macbeth's integrity by praising him, he regains a degree of intellectual control (F #8, 7/3)

- finally, having made statements throughout the speech so far, Lenox finally turns to direct questioning - and as he does so full intellectual control is lost, replaced first by passion (F #9, 2/3) as he indirectly asks confirmation of Macduffe's whereabouts, and then byemotion as he asks more directly (F #10, 0/2)

- interestingly, the decision to do this seems to be difficult for him for the first phrase of F #9 is set as a very short, monosyllabic, emotional (via the only semicolon in the speech) surround phrase ' . But peace ; ' – though whether this is intended for his colleague because he has offended him or for himself to calm himself down is up to each actor to explore

The Tragedie of Macbeth

Rosse

I have words/That would be howl'd out in the desert ayre,
between 4.3.193 - 207

Background: Rosse has come to England on a double mission - to add his voice in bringing Malcome back to Scotland and to give the appalling news to Macduff of his family's slaughter. Having put the second task off for some time, Rosse finally begins to break the news.

Style: one on one address with a third person present

Where: somewhere in the English court

To Whom: Macduff, in front of Malcome

# of Lines: 12

Probable Timing: 0.40 minutes

Rosse

1　　　　　　　I have words
　　　That would be howl'd out in the desert air,
　　　Where hearing should not latch them .

2　　No mind that's honest
　　　But in it shares some woe, though the main part
　　　Pertains to you alone .

3　　Let not your ears despise my tongue for ever,
　　　Which shall possess them with the heaviest sound
　　　That ever yet they heard .

4　　Your castle is surpris'd ; your wife, and babes
　　　Savagely slaughter'd .

5　　　　　　　　　To relate the manner,
　　　Were on the quarry of these [murder'd] deer
　　　To add the death of you .

Rosse

1   I have words
        That would be howl'd out in the desert ayre,
        Where hearing should not latch them .

---

2   No minde that's honest
        But in it shares some woe, though the maine part
        Pertaines to you alone .

---

3   Let not your eares dispise my tongue for ever,
        Which shall possesse them with the heaviest sound
        That ever yet they heard .

---

4   Your Castle is surpriz'd : your Wife, and Babes
        Savagely slaughter'd : To relate the manner
        Were on the Quarry of these [murther'd] Deere
        To adde the death of you .

• that Rosse is attempting to keep himself in check can be seen in F #1's set-up to the bad news

" I have words/That would be howl'd out in the desert ayre, /Where hearing should not latch them."
which is unembellished save for the one word 'ayre'

• that, understandably, he cannot stay unemotional can be seen in the next two sentences, both in F #2's suggesting that the news 'Pertaines to you alone' (0/3) and F #3's apology for what he is about to say (0/2)

• and then his style completely changes as he begins to report the horrors, becoming intellectual (F #4, 6/3) with the voicing of the dreadful

" . Your Castle is surpriz'd :your Wife, and Babes/Savagely slaughter'd :"

heightened by being set as two successive surround phrases - whether as an attempt not to let himself be swamped by the information or to ensure that he can make the briefness of each point tell without unnecessary elaboration is up to each actor to explore

The Life of Timon of Athens

Timon

Oh no doubt my good Friends, but the Gods
1.2.88 - 108

Background: at one of his frequent almost potlatch-type banquets, Timon gives praise to his friends; as such, and as an explanation of his personal philosophy, the speech is self-explanatory: that then text is in prose might well suggest he is overcome by the enormity of the gracious praise (lip-service as it eventually turns out) which has triggered this speech

Style: general address to a large group

Where: Timon's home

To Whom: a large number of guests

# of Lines: 20

Probable Timing: 1.00 minutes

Timon

1   O, no doubt, my good friends, but the gods
    themselves have provided that I shall have much help
    from you :how had you been my friends else ?

2   Why
    have you that charitable title from thousands, did not
    you chiefly belong to my heart ?

3   I have told more of
    you to myself, [than] you can with modesty speak in
    your own behalf;and thus far I confirm you .

4   O
    you gods, think I, what need we have any friends, if
    we should ne'er have need of 'em ?

5   They were the most
    needless creatures living, should we ne'er have use for
    'em; and would most resemble sweet instruments
    hung up in cases, that keeps their sounds to them-
    selves .

6   Why I have often wish'd myself poorer, that
    I might come nearer to you .

7   We are borne to do bene-
    fits ; and what better or properer can we call our own
    [than] the riches of our friends ?

8   O, what a precious com-
    fort 'tis, to have so many like brothers commanding
    one another's fortunes !

9   O, [joy e'en made away ere't
    can be born !]

10   Mine eyes cannot hold out water, methinks .

11 To forget their faults, I drink to you .

Timon

1   Oh no doubt my good Friends, but the Gods
themselves have provided that I shall have much helpe
from you :how had you beene my Friends else .

2   Why
have you that charitable title from thousands ?

3   Did not
you chiefely belong to my heart ?

4   I have told more of
you to my selfe, [then] you can with modestie speake in
your owne behalfe .

5   And thus farre I confirme you .

6   Oh
you Gods (thinke I,) what need we have any Friends; if
we should nere have need of 'em ?

7   They were the most
needlesse Creatures living; should we nere have use for
'em ?

8   And would most resemble sweete Instruments
hung up in Cases, that keepes there sounds to themselves .

9   Why I have often wisht my selfe poorer, that
I might come neerer to you :we are borne to do benefits .

10   And what better or properer can we call our owne,
[then] the riches of our Friends ?

11   Oh what a pretious comfort 'tis, to have so many like Brothers commanding
one anothers Fortunes .

12   Oh [joyes, e'ne made away er't
can be borne]: mine eies cannot hold out water me thinks
to forget their Faults .

13   I drinke to you .

• Timon's philosophy of friendship, that is to be so rudely shattered later in the play, is underscored by four consecutive emotional surround phrases created by the only semicolons in the speech

" . Oh you Gods (thinke I,) what need we have any Friends ; if we should nere have need of 'em ? They were the most needlesse Creatures living ; should we nere have use for 'em ? "

while the pleasure such friendship yields is neatly encapsulated in the logical (colon created) surround phrases

" . Why I have often wisht my selfe poorer, that I might come neerer to you : we are borne to do benefits."

" . Oh joyes, e'ne made away er't can be borne : mine eies cannot hold out water me thinks to forget their Faults . "

• his opening passionate belief (F #1, 3/3) that friends are provided by 'the Gods' is heightened by the first surround phrase of the speech ' : how had you beene my Friends else . ' – which is offered as a statement, not as a question as most modern texts show, adding a question mark to the end of mt. #1 suggest

• the fact that F's sentence that follows, striking in its calmness

"Why have you that charitable title from thousands?"

is not only the sole unembellished passage in the speech but is also regarded by most modern texts as ungrammatical (and therefore rationally joined with the sentence that follows) suggests Timon is so moved by the idea of friendship and the number of friends present that it is difficult for him to even speak the thought

• but then as Timon confirms those present as belonging to his heart (F #3-5) he becomes highly emotional (0/6 in two and a half lines)

• the emotional surround phrase lead-in to and the celebration of the need for friends turns passionate (5/5, F #6-8), as does the somewhat naive F #10-11 belief how wonderful it is so many 'Brothers' are able to command 'one anothers Fortunes' (3/2)

• though in the midst of this passion both the corollary that he has often wished himself poorer to take advantage of their friendship (F #9) and the peculiarly ungrammatical finale offering breathing/thinking proof of just how moved/disturbed he is as he tries to drink away his joys and tears (F #12-13) are very emotional (0/3, 1/5 respectively)

The Life of Timon of Athens

Steward

Lord Lucius and Lucullus, {and the Senators}?   Humh.
between 2.2.196 - 213

Background: having accepted that he is in financial trouble, Timon
has decided to dispatch several trusted servants to his closest
friends and Senators, all of whom have benefited from his enormous generosity, asking for financial help: however, his personal
philosophy as expounded in speech #1 does not seem to be shared
by others the Steward has so far approached on Timon's behalf

Style: as part of a two-handed scene

Where: outside, close to Timon's home

To Whom: his employer,

# of Lines: 15

Probable Timing: 0.50 minutes

Steward

1   Lord Lucius and Lucullus ,{and the Senators}?

2   Humh !

---

3   I have been bold
     (For that I knew it the most general way)
     To them to use your signet, and your name,
     But they do shake their heads, and I am here
     No richer in return .

---

4   They answer, in a joint and corporate voice,
     That now they are at fall, want treasure, cannot
     Do what they would, are sorry;you are honorable,
     But yet they could have wish'd - they know not -
     Something hath been amiss - a noble nature
     May catch a wrench - would all were well - tis pity -
     And so, intending other serious matters,
     After distasteful looks - and these hard fractions,
     With certain half-caps and cold-moving nods,
     They froze me into silence .

Steward

1   Lord Lucius and Lucullus ,{and the Senators}?

2   Humh .

---

3   I have beene bold
     (For that I knew it the most generall way)
     To them, to use your Signet, and your Name,
     But they do shake their heads, and I am heere
     No richer in returne .

---

4   They answer in a joynt and corporate voice,
     That now they are at fall, want Tre aure cannot
     Do what they would, are sorrie : you are Honourable,
     But yet they could have wisht, they know not,
     Something hath beene amisse ; a Noble Nature
     May catch a wrench ; would all were well ; tis pitty,
     And so intending other serious matters,
     After distastefull lookes; and these hard Fractions
     With certaine halfe-caps, and cold moving nods,
     They froze me into Silence .

• the Steward's initial put down of those Timon has suggested contacting for help is totally intellectual (F #1, 3/0), followed by F #2's unembellished one word monosyllabic release – the orthography suggesting whatever the 'Humh' signifies it be done quietly, almost as if for the Steward's benefit alone

• the Steward's explanation that he has already approached them in Timon's name is emotional (F #3, 2/4)

• initially his report of their answer is careful, just one intellectual release pointing to their proffered reasons for refusal (lack of 'Treasure') and the fact everyone answered as one 'joynt' voice (1/1, F #4's first two and a half lines)

• however his reporting of their avowals of respect for Timon turn emotional (1/3, the next two lines), and as he continues his report, so his control is put to the test as testified by the two emotional surround phrases (unusually heightened by being formed by three successive semicolons, a great rarity in any original Shakespeare printing)

" ; a Noble Nature/May catch a wrench ; would all were well ; "

and the emotion is maintained through the remainder of the speech as he describes how after all the fine words he was dismissed with 'distastefull lookes' (this description heightened further by being punctuated with the final semicolon of the passage) and 'cold moving nods' (2/5, the last four lines of the speech)

The Life of Timon of Athens

Apermantus

This is in thee a Nature but infected,

4.3.202 - 218

Background: Apermantus is rightly known by all as a cynic; even in his better times Timon has publicly acknowledged that Apermantus 'does neither affect companie/Nor is he fit for't indeed': yet Apermantus was concerned for Timon from the start, 'Oh you Gods!What a number of men eats, and he sees 'em not? ': now, in Timon's self-imposed impoverished exile 'Nothing Ile beare from thee /But nakednesse, thou detestable Towne', Apermantus has joined him in the woods, not to comfort him but to strip him of any self-deception: the two following speeches come from the beginning of the in-the-woods encounter, and as such, each is self-explanatory

Style: each as part of a two-handed scene

Where: at Timon's camp in the woods

To Whom: Timon

# of Lines: 17

Probable Timing: 0.55 minutes

Take Note: With thirty-three releases in just seventeen lines it seems that Apermantus is not holding back in letting Timon know what he thinks about his new behaviour – whether this is because his own status as the local misanthrope is challenged, or an attempt to shock Timon back to reality out of a grudging affection for him, or simply because he must speak his mind no matter what the circumstances, is up to each actor to explore.

Apermantus

1   This is in thee a nature but infected,
    A poor unmanly melancholy sprung
    From change of future .

2   Why this spade ? this place ?
    This slave-like habit ? and these looks of care ?

3   Thy flatterers yet wear silk, drink wine, lie soft,
    Hug their diseas'd perfumes, and have forgot
    That ever Timon was .

4   Shame not these woods
    By putting on the cunning of a carper .

5   Be thou a flatterer now, and seek to thrive
    By that which has undone thee ;hinge thy knee,
    And let his very breath whom thou'lt observe
    Blow off thy cap, praise his most vicious strain,
    And call it excellent .

6   Thou wast told thus ;
    Thou gav'st thine ears (like tapsters that [bade] welcome)
    To knaves, and all approachers .

7   'Tis most just
    That thou turn rascal; hadst thou wealth again,
    Rascals should have't .

8   Do not assume my likeness.

Apermantus

1 This is in thee a Nature but infected,
A poore unmanly Melancholly sprung
From change of future .

2   Why this Spade ? this place ?
This Slave-like Habit, and these lookes of Care ?

3 Thy Flatterers yet weare Silke, drinke Wine, lye soft,
Hugge their diseas'd Perfumes, and have forgot
That ever Timon was .

4   Shame not these Woods,
By putting on the cunning of a Carper .

5 Be thou a Flatterer now, and seeke to thrive
By that which ha's undone thee ;hindge thy knee,
And let his very breath whom thou'lt observe
Blow off thy Cap : praise his most vicious straine,
And call it excellent :thou wast told thus :
Thou gav'st thine eares (like Tapsters, that [bad] welcom)
To Knaves, and all approachers :'Tis most just
That thou turne Rascall, had'st thou wealth againe,
Rascals should have't .

6   Do not assume my likenesse .

· Apermantus is passionate in ascribing Timon's change as one of infection or 'Melancholly' rather than a true change of heart (2/2, F #1)

· F #2's challenge of what on earth he is doing dressed as he is, where he is (with just a spade) is ferociously intellectual (4/1 in two lines)

· F #3's (deliberately tantalising? cruel?) suggestion that Timon's one-time Flatterers, still living in the lap of luxury, have forgotten him is passionate (5/4), while calling out Timon to stop his pretence is cuttingly intellectual (2/0, F #4)

· and then Apermantus loses some control, for his F #5 jamming together of instructions how to resolve Timon's current situation, plus the told-you-so, and your-fate-is-well-deserved taunt. is not only on-rushed – most modern texts reworking it as three more rational sentences – it opens with an emotional (semicoloned) surround phrase telling him to become a 'Flatterer' to undo the damage done to him (by his flatterers!)

· F #5's passionate start (2/3, the first four and half lines) ends with an ugly surround phrase suggestion as how to respond to his flatterers ' : praise his most vicious straine,/And call it excellent : '

· after the icily unembellished ' : thou wast told thus : ', doubly heightened by being set as a monosyllabic surround phrase, Apermantus' passions flow once more (4/5) as he finishes ripping Timon apart, the brevity of the bluntness of the final 'Do not assume my likenesse.' seems to suggest this warning is much more than a casual comment or joke

The Life of Timon of Athens

Timon

Would'st thou have thy selfe fall in the confusion
between 4.3.234 - 345

Background: Timon eventually gives as good as he gets: having
asked Apermantus what he would do with the world 'if it lay in
thy power?' and received the answer 'Give it to the Beasts, to be
rid of the men', Timon in turn strips Apermantus of the
sense-of-unique-superiority he clings to

Style: as part of a two-handed scene

Where: at Timon's camp in the woods

To Whom: Apermantus

# of Lines: 21

Probable Timing: 1.10 minutes

Take Note: This is one of the rare times F sets more sentences than
its modern counterpart, (what most modern texts set as an onrushed mt. #3 was originally set as four F sentences). However, F's
divisions are not so much grammatical, since all four sentences essentially deal with Apermantus' inevitable failure to survive no
matter what form of animal he would choose to be. Rather each
new F sentence seems to mark a different internal response from
Timon (and hence change in stylistic release) to what he, in turn,
is now piling onto/stripping away from Apermantus' own self-de-
lusion.

Timon

1   Wouldst thou have thyself fall in the confu-
    sion of men, and remain a beast with the beasts?

---

2   A beastly ambition, which the gods grant
    thee t'attain to !

3   If thou wert the lion, the fox would
    beguile thee ;if thou wert the lamb, the fox would
    eat thee ;if thou wert the fox, the lion would suspect
    thee, when peradventure thou wert accus'd by the ass;
    if thou wert the ass, thy dullness would torment thee,
    and still thou liv'dst but as a breakfast to the wolf ; if
    thou wert the wolf, thy greediness would afflict thee,
    & oft thou shouldst hazard thy life for thy dinner ; wert
    thou the unicorn, pride and wrath would confound
    thee and make thine own self the conquest of thy fury ;
    wert thou a bear, thou wouldst be kill'd by the horse ;
    wert thou a horse, thou wouldst be seiz'd by the leo-
    pard ;wert thou a leopard, thou wert germane to the
    lion, and the spots of thy kindred, were jurors on thy
    life ; all thy safety were remotion and thy defense ab-
    sence .

4   What beast could'st thou be, that were not sub-
    ject to a beast ?

5   And what a beast art thou already, that
    seest not thy loss in transformation !

Timon

1 Would'st thou have thy selfe fall in the confusion of men, and remaine a Beast with the Beasts .

---

2 A beastly Ambition, which the Goddes graunt
thee t'attaine to .

3   If thou wert the Lyon, the Fox would
beguile thee, if thou wert the Lambe, the Foxe would
eate thee : if thou wert the Fox, the Lion would suspect
thee, when peradventure thou wert accus'd by the Asse :
If thou wert the Asse, thy dulnesse would torment thee ;
and still thou liv'dst but as a Breakefast to the Wolfe .

4   If
thou wert the Wolfe, thy greedinesse would afflict thee,
& oft thou should'st hazard thy life for thy dinner .

5   Wert
thou the Unicorne, pride and wrath would confound
thee, and make thine owne selfe the conquest of thy fury .

6 Wert thou a Beare, thou would'st be kill'd by the Horse :
wert thou a Horse, thou would'st be seaz'd by the Leopard : wert thou a Leopard, thou wert Germane to the
Lion, and the spottes of thy Kindred, were Jurors on thy
life .

7   All thy safety were remotion, and thy defence ab-
sense .

8   What Beast could'st thou bee, that were not subject to a Beast :and what a Beast art thou already, that
seest not thy losse in transformation .

• with all that has been dumped on him by Apermantus (see speeches #9-10 above) it's not surprising that Timon starts out so passionately (15/11, in just the first nine lines, F #1-3), and amidst all the insults it's fascinating that the end of the passion, which focuses essentially on Apermantus' intelligence, or lack thereof, is enhanced even further by being set as two surround phrases,

> " : If thou wert the Asse, thy dulnesse would torment thee ; and still thou liv'dst but as a Breakefast to the Wolfe."
>
> their conviction heightened even further by the only emotional semicolon of the speech that links them

• for a moment, as Timon turns to the deadly sins of greed and pride, he becomes quite emotional (2/5, F #4-5)

• and then, as he turns his attention to the possibility of Apermantus' death, he manages to regain his self-control (F #6, 9/4)

• and just as Apermantus went deadly quiet in giving what he thought would be Timon's coup-de-grace in the previous speech so Timon follows suit, with F #7's

> "All thy safety were remotion, and thy defence absense.'

• while F #8's final triumphant surround phrase flourish becomes passionate once more (#3/2)

The Tragedie of King Lear
Edmund/Bastard
Thou Nature art my Goddesse, to thy Law
1.2.1 - 22

Background: also known as the Bastard, this is the illegitimate Edmund's first major speech: given the fact that being the elder brother, had he been legitimate he would be the first in line to inherit from his father (together with the jokes made in front of him to Kent about there being 'good sport at his making, and the horson must be acknowledged') the determination in the speech is very understandable

Style: solo

Where: unspecified, but probably Gloucester's home

To Whom: direct audience address and self

# of Lines: 22

Probable Timing: 1.10 minutes

Edmund

1   Thou, Nature, art my goddess, to thy law
    My services are bound .

2   Wherefore should I
    Stand in the plague of custom, and permit
    The curiosity of nations, to deprive me,
    For that I am some twelve or fourteen moonshines
    Lag of a brother?

4   Why bastard?

5   Wherefore base?

6   When my dimensions are as well compact,
    My mind is generous, and my shape as true,
    As honest madam's issue?

7   Why brand they us
    With base? with baseness bastardy? base, base?

8   Who, in the lusty stealth of nature, take
    More composition, and fierce quality,
    [Than] doth within a dull, stale, tired bed
    Go to th'creating a whole tribe of fops,
    Got 'tween asleep and wake?

9   Well then,
    Legitimate Edgar, I must have your land .

10 Our father's love is to the bastard Edmund
    As to th'legitimate.

11   Fine word: legitimate !

12 Well, my legitimate, if this letter speed
    And my invention thrive, [Edmund] the base
    Shall [top] 'th'legitimate.

13   I grow, I prosper:
    Now, gods, stand up for bastards !

Bastard

1   Thou Nature art my Goddesse, to thy Law
    My services are bound, wherefore should I
    Stand in the plague of custome, and permit
    The curiosity of Nations, to deprive me?

2   For that I am some twelve, or fourteene Moonshines
    Lag of a Brother?

3   Why Bastard?

4   Wherefore base?

5   When my Dimensions are as well compact,
    My minde is generous, and my shape as true
    As honest Madams issue?

6   Why brand they us
    With Base?

7   With basenes Barstadie?

8   Base, Base?

9   Who in the lustie stealth of Nature, take
    More composition, and fierce qualitie,
    [Then] doth within a dull stale tyred bed
    Goe to th'creating a whole tribe of Fops
    Got 'tweene a sleepe, and wake?

10   Well then,
    Legitimate Edgar, I must have your land,
    Our Fathers love, is to the Bastard Edmond,
    As to th'legitimate: fine word: Legitimate.

11 Well, my Legittimate, if this Letter speed,
    And my invention thrive, [Edmond] the base
    Shall[to]'th'Legitimate: I grow, I prosper:
    Now Gods, stand up for Bastards.

- while the three sentence lead in to the all important question, why should he and all that should be his (at least in his own eyes) be dismissed through the term 'Bastard' is firmly intellectual (7/3, F #1-3), the urgency of the question rides rough-shod over syntactical niceties . . .

- . . . for as set, F #1 is not grammatical: the pledging of himself to nature slips within the same sentence (via a fast-link comma) to his very dangerous challenge (in Elizabethan eyes) to conventional social order – and F's drive is very understandable in human terms, yet most modern texts replace the comma by a period, thus starting the question far more rationally

- and thus, according to most modern texts, F #2 is also ungrammatical: however, as reset in most modern texts it simply continues to expand upon the question already asked, but as set in F, this new sentence in fact answers F #1's rhetorical question with some form of emphasis (with ridicule? scorn? certainly decisively) – the function of the Elizabethan question mark is that it can serve as an exclamation point

- it would seen that the low status associated with bastardy disturbs him, for the unembellished short F #4 'Wherefore base?' is very quiet, whether in an attempt to control emotion (little of which has been seen so far in the speech) or out of genuine pain and hurt is up to each actor to explore

- the assertion of himself as equal in every respect to 'honest Madams issue' starts out intellectually (5/2, F 5-8), despite the repetition of the (troubling?) 'Base' ending the sequence, but as he expands on how it takes 'More composition, and fierce qualitie' to create a bastard than in creating lawfully 'a whole tribe of Fops' so he becomes passionate (2/3, F #9)

- and then comes the switch that if any on-stage character were to overhear would cause them great concern, for the two sentence naked plotting to have Edgar's birthright (F #10-11) is not only far less held in check than most modern texts' rational six sentence setting (suggesting Edmund is riding almost unfettered the wild horses of his desire), it is also relentlessly intellectual (11/1, the last seven and a half lines of the speech)

- and at last, the determined surround phrases make their appearance, adding almost celebratory weight to his thinking, with

" : fine word : Legitimate . "

" : I grow, I prosper : Now Gods, stand up for Bastards . "

The Tragedie of King Lear
Kent

Fellow I know thee ./{Thou'rt a}Knave, a Rascall, ,
between 2.2.13 - 24

Background: Lear has sent Kent/Caius to Gloucester's palace where
unbeknownst to him both Cornwall and Regan are journeying:
so that Regan will know her mind , and that the plot to strip Lear
of large numbers of his train has begun, Gonerill has sent letters
by her steward Oswald, who naturally has followed Regan and
Cornwall to Gloucester's home: there Kent/Caius and Oswald
meet once more, Kent having tripped him up and beaten him earlier for rudeness to Lear: Kent recognises Oswald, who does not
immediately recognise him in return: here, a series of neutral
questions from Oswald have been answered rudely by Kent/Caius,
generating the Steward's reasonable question, 'Why do'st thou use
me thus? I know thee not', which triggers the following

Style: as part of a two-handed scene

Where: the courtyard of Gloucester's palace

To Whom: Gonerill's steward, Oswald

# of Lines: 11

Probable Timing: 0.40 minutes

Kent

1   Fellow, I know thee.

---

2   {Thou'rt a} knave, a rascal, an eater of broken meats;
     a base, proud, shallow, beggarly, three-suited hundred-
     pound, filthy worsted-stocking knave ; a lily-livered,
     action-taking, whoreson, glass-gazing, super serviceable,
     finical rogue ; one trunk-inheriting slave ; one that
     wouldst be a bawd in a way of good service, and art no-
     thing but the composition of a knave, beggar, coward,
     pandar, and the son and heir of a mongrel bitch ;
     one whom I will beat into [clamorous] whining, if thou
     deni'st the least syllable of thy addition .

Kent

1   Fellow I know thee.

---

2   {Thou'rt a} Knave, a Rascall, an eater of broken meates,
     a base, proud, shallow, beggerly, three-suited- hundred
     pound, filthy woosted-stocking knave, a Lilly-livered,
     action-taking, whoreson glasse-gazing super-serviceable
     finicall Rogue, one Trunke-inheriting slave, one that
     would'st be a Baud in a way of good service, and art no-
     thing but the composition of a Knave, Begger, Coward,
     Pandar, and the Sonne and Heire of a Mungrill Bitch,
     one whom I will beate into [clamours] whining, if thou
     deny'st the least sillable of thy addition .

- Kent's opening short sentence unembellished calm is highly deceptive
- for the explosive F #2 (14/11 in just ten lines) runs the gamut of insulting styles

  a/ the one line suggestion that the Steward is so low in the pecking order all he eats are scraps left over after others have eaten, is passionate (2/2)

  b/ that his clothing is that of a servant rather than the higher rank of Steward is quietly emotional (0/1)

  c/ that his nature is that of a 'Lilly-livered ... Baud' is passionate (4/3)

  d/ that all his pedigree adds up to is a 'Mungrell Bitch' is highly intellectual/factual (8/3)

- the whole ending with the emotional threat of a beating (0/2), until, as the speech opened, the sudden (and presumably very dangerous) unembellished calm of the last phrase

      "if thou deny'st the least sillable of thy addition'

The Tragedie of King Lear

Fool/Foole

And thou hadst beene set i'th'Stockes for that
between 2.4.64 - 85

Background: Kent/Caius' anger with Oswald spilled over to insulting both Cornwall and Regan when they arrived to prevent him from beating Oswald yet again: as a result, and despite his protests that he is a representative of the king, Kent has been imprisoned in the stocks overnight: Lear has arrived, but Gonerill's insistence that he reduce his attendant knights has already had effect, for many of his supporters did not make the journey with him: thus the still stocked Kent asks the Foole, 'How chance the king comes with so small a number?', to which the Foole answers thus

Style: as part of a three-handed scene

Where: in the courtyard of Gloucester's palace

To Whom: Kent, in front of Lear's Gentleman

# of Lines: 18

Probable Timing: 0.55 minutes

Take Note: Though the speech is highly emotional (5/21 overall), the unembellished lines point to the deeper political message beneath his surface fooling.

Fool

1   And thou hadst been set i'th'stocks for that
      question, thou'dst well deserv'd it .

---

2   All that follow their
      noses are led by their eyes but blind men, and there's
      not a nose among twenty but can smell him that's stink-
      ing .

3   Let go thy hold when a great wheel runs down a
      hill, lest it break thy neck with following ;but the
      great one that goes upward, let him draw thee after .

4   When a wise man gives thee better counsel, give me mine
      again, I would [have] none but knaves follow it, since a
      fool gives it .

5   That sir, which serves and seeks for gain,
                  And follows but for form,
                  Will pack, when it begins to rain,
                  And leave thee in the storm .

6   But I will tarry, the fool will stay,
                  And let the wise man fly .

7   The knave turns fool that runs away,
                  The Fool no knave, perdie .

Foole

1   And thou hadst beene set i'th'Stockes for that
    question, thoud'st well deserv'd it .

---

2   All that follow their
    noses, are led by their eyes, but blinde men, and there's
    not a nose among twenty, but can smell him that's stink-
    ing ; let go thy hold, when a great wheele runs downe a
    hill, least it breake thy necke with following .

3   But the
    great one that goes upward, let him draw thee after :
    when a wiseman gives thee better counsell give me mine
    againe, I would [hause] none but knaves follow it, since a
    Foole gives it .

4   That Sir, which serves and seekes for gaine,
                    And followes but for forme ;
                    Will packe, when it begins to raine,
                    And leave thee in the storme,
                    But I will tarry, the Foole will stay,
                    And let the wiseman flie :
                    The knave turnes Foole that runnes away,
                    The Foole no knave perdie .

"and there's not a nose among twenty, but can smell him that's

   stinking;"

   which is then followed by an emotionally enhanced (by the semicolon) emotionally released surround phrase of explanation (0/4)

" ; let go thy hold, when a great wheele runs downe a hill, least it

breake thy necke with following . "

   with the astute logical outcome heightened by being offered as both unembellished and a surround phrase

" . But the great one that goes upward, let him draw thee after : "

- the Foole opens fairly calmly if slightly emotionally (1/3, the first four lines), but his emotions intensify with 'the great wheele runs downe' it will 'breake thy necke' (0/4, F #2's last two lines)

- the unembellished advice to follow a 'great one' is followed by an emotional kick as to the value of a Foole's advice being better than that of a 'wiseman' (1/3, F #3's last two and half lines)

- with the final doggerel of F #4 being onrushed it seems that the rise and fall of great ones and their followers is disturbing to him – the first four lines referring to fair-weather followers who will leave at the first sign of trouble being very emotional (1/6), while the last four lines praising (his own?) loyalty no matter what is passionate (3/4): F 4#'s onrush suggests this could well be an improvised piece – by splitting it into three more rational sentences, however, most modern texts seem to have set it as a well crafted ditty (perhaps already composed by another)

The Tragedie of King Lear
Fool/Foole

This is a brave night to coole a Curtizan:
3.2.79 - 96

Background: Caius, the disguised Kent, has sought and found Lear and the Foole on the heath, and urges them to take shelter; he and Lear have left the stage, leaving the Foole alone to utter the following

Style: solo

Where: the heath

To Whom: direct audience address

# of Lines: 16

Probable Timing: 0.50 minutes

Take Note: At last this seems to be the outburst that the smaller political statements embedded in more general fooling in earlier speeches seen earlier have been threatening .

Fool

1   This is a brave night to cool a courtezan .

2   I'll speak a prophecy ere I go :
    When priests are more in word, [than] matter ;
    When brewers mar their malt with water ;
    When [tailors are their nobles tutors] ;
    No heretics burn'd, but wenches' suitors;
    Then shall the realm of Albion
    Come into great confusion .

3   When every case in law is right ;
    No squire in debt, nor no poor knight ;
    When slanders do not live in tongues ;
    Nor cut purses come not to throngs ;
    When usurers tell their gold i'th'field,
    And bawds and whores, do churches build ;
    Then comes the time, who lives to see't,
    That going shall be us'd with feet .

4   This prophecy Merlin shall make, for I live before
            his time

Foole

1 This is a brave night to coole a Curtizan :
   Ile speake a Prophesie ere I go :
   When Priests are more in word, [then] matter ;
   When Brewers marre their Malt with water ;
   When [Nobles are their Taylors Tutors],
   No Heretiques burn'd but wenches Sutors ;
   When every Case in Law, is right ;
   No Squire in debt, nor no poore Knight ;
   When Slanders do not live in Tongues ;
   Nor Cut-purses come not to throngs ;
   When Usurers tell their Gold i'th'Field,
   And Baudes, and whores, do Churches build,
   Then shal the Realme of Albion, come to great confusion :
   Then comes the time, who lives to see't,
   That going shalbe us'd with feet .

2 This prophecie Merlin shall make, for I live before his time .

That it is not as foolish or as innocent a piece of doggerel as is often played, can be seen in . . .

  a/ the onrush of F #2 (split into two more rational sentences in most modern texts)
  b/ the enormous intellectualism of the speech (24/6 overall)
  c/ half the sixteen lines are set as determined surround phrases
  d/ six of which are further heightened by (emotional) semicolons
  e/ after all the excesses, the final gloomy three line prophecy of England declining to the point that 'going shalbe us'd with feet' is essentially unembellished - with the name 'Merlin' being the only release in (the undercutting/self-excusing/I'm-not-saying-this-but-somebody-else-will) F#2
• that this notion is so disturbing to him can be seen the shaded F only line

"Then shal the Realme of Albion, come to great confusion'

being overlylong (13 syllables at least), seeming to underscore the Foole's passionate overflow of feeling as he contemplates England's destruction: however, not only do most modern texts split this F only line in two, so as to maintain the doggerel/'songspiel' style of the speech, as shown, some move it away from the climactic F placement to a weaker position ending the to them more rational setting at the end of their mt. #1

Brutus

All tongues speake of him, and the bleared sights
between 2.1.205 - 223

Background: to satisfy the rebellious people, five Tribunes, or represen-
tatives, have been appointed to speak on their behalf: this does not
sit well with Martius whose reaction was, 'Sdeath,/the rabble should
first have unroo'(f)t the city/Ere so prevayl'd with me;': that it does
not sit well with Martius, and like thinkers, is well known to two of
the Tribunes, Brutus who here is analysing the situation with his colleague Sicinius; the 'him' spoken of in the first line is Martius, who
has returned to Rome with a hero's welcome, receiving the 'Oaken
Garland' for the third time, and adding to his name Caius Martius
'Coriolanus', a name to celebrate and commemorate his single-handed
capture of the Volscian city of Corioles

Style: as part of a two-handed scene

Where: a Roman street

To Whom: a fellow Tribune Sicinius

# of Lines: 19

Probable Timing: 1.00 minutes

Take Note: F's onrushed F #2 (split into two more rational litanies of
complaint by most modern texts) and two (shaded) passages of irregular lines imply a character not in full control of himself – and the orthography suggests when the breakdown occurs, once Brutus begins
to describe how everywhere everyone is 'In earnestnesse to see him'.

Brutus

1 All tongues speak of him, and the bleared sights
   Are spectacled to see him .

2   Your prattling nurse
   Into a rapture lets her baby cry
   While she chats him ; the kitchen malkin pins
   Her richest lockram 'bout her reechy neck,
   Clamb'ring the walls to eye him ;stalls, bulks, windows,
   Are smother'd up, leads fill'd, and ridges hors'd
   With variable complexions, all agreeing
   In earnestness to see him .

3   Seld-shown flamens
   Do press among the popular throngs, and puff
   To win a vulgar station ; our veil'd dames
   Commit the war of white and damask in
   Their nicely gawded cheeks toth'wanton spoil
   Of Phoebus' burning kisses - such a pother
   As if that whatsoever god, who leads him
   Were slily crept into his human powers,
   And gave him graceful posture .

4{} Our office may, during his power, go sleep

Brutus

1   All tongues speake of him, and the bleared sights
Are spectacled to see him .

2   Your pratling Nurse
Into a rapture lets her Baby crie,
While she chats him : the Kitchin Malkin pinnes
Her richest Lockram 'bout her reechie necke,
Clambring the Walls to eye him :
Stalls, Bulkes, Windowes, are smother'd up,
Leades fill'd, and Ridges hors'd
With variable Complexions ; all agreeing
In earnestnesse to see him : seld-showne Flamins
Doe presse among the popular Throngs, and puffe
To winne a vulgar station : our veyl'd Dames
Commit the Warre of White and Damaske
In their nicely gawded Cheekes, toth'wanton spoyle
Of Phoebus burning Kisses : such a poother,
As if that whatsoever God, who leades him,
Were slyly crept into his humane powers,
And gave him gracefull posture .

3{}   Our Office may, during his power, goe sleepe .

• with its very quiet start (F #1 slightly emotional, 0/1, F#2's first two lines slightly intellectual, 2/0) it seems that Brutus is just beginning to notice what is taking place around them, or, given the excesses later in the speech, is trying very hard not to let his antipathy towards Coriolanus get in the way of analysing the current political danger

• but as Brutus describes how even the lowest are dressing up to see Coriolanus, so his releases start to flow, though he still manages some self control (4/2 in just F #2's next two lines, between the first two colons) a control undercut by being set as three irregular lines (7/8/6 syllables suggesting Brutus struggles to retain self-composure)

• and then, as he describes/imagines people scrambling to see Coriolanus from every possible vantage point, so his full flow turns passionate (4/4, the next three and half lines), leading to the only surround phrase in the speech

" ; all agreeing/In earnestnesse to see him : "

heightened by starting with the only emotional semi-colon in the speech

• the fact that even Priests ('Flamins') are struggling with the 'popular Throngs' creates an (amazed? horrified? despairing?) emotional response, (2/5, F #2's next two lines), while the observation that the better sort of women ('our veyl'd Dames' are attracted towards Coriolanus triggers an enormously passionate reaction (7/7 in just the next three lines) - the slightly irregular structure 9/11 syllables) showing another imbalance as he describes the women's reactions

• and his accurate summation that since Coriolanus is now being idolized as something more than human their new 'Office' may 'goe sleepe' is highly emotional once more (2/5, the last four and half lines of the speech)

The Tragedy of Coriolanus

Coriolanus

You common cry of Curs, whose breath I hate,
3.3.118 - 135

Background: all the appeasing advice has gone for naught, for once
in the market place Coriolanus' short temper has got the best of
him again, and he has insulted both the people and the Tribunes,
yet again: Sicinius has therefore pronounced Coriolanus' exile, or
worse ('In the name a'th'people,/And in the power of us the Tribunes, wee/(Ev'n from this instant) banish him our Citie/In
perill of precipitation/From off the Rocke Tarpeian, never more/
To enter our Rome gates./I'th'Peoples name,/I say it shall bee so):
the following is Coriolanus' reply

Style: public address

Where: the Market-place

To Whom: all present, supporters and foes alike

# of Lines: 16

Probable Timing: 0.50 minutes

Take Note: Having been tricked into anger, far from abasing himself,
Coriolanus' initiates an unrelenting passionate attack (13/15 overall), and though seemingly logical, F's orthography reveals two
rather surprising moments at speech's end.

Coriolanus

1　You common cry of curs, whose breath I hate
　As reek a'th'rotten fens, whose loves I prize
　As the dead carcasses of unburied men
　That do corrupt my air - I banish you !
　And here remain with your uncertainty!

2　Let every feeble rumor shake your hearts !
　Your enemies, with nodding of their plumes,
　Fan you into despair !

3　Have the power still
　To banish your defenders, till at length
　Your ignorance (which finds not till it feels,
　Making but reservation of yourselves,
　Still your own foes) deliver you as most
　Abated captives to some nation
　That won you without blows!

4　　　　　　　　　　　　　　Despising,
　For you, the city, thus I turn my back;
　There is a world elsewhere .

Coriolanus

1   You common cry of Curs, whose breath I hate,
    As reeke a'th'rotten Fennes : whose Loves I prize,
    As the dead Carkasses of unburied men,
    That do corrupt my Ayre : I banish you,
    And heere remaine with your uncertaintie .

2   Let every feeble Rumor shake your hearts :
    Your Enemies, with nodding of their Plumes
    Fan you into dispaire : Have the power still
    To banish your Defenders, till at length
    Your ignorance (which findes not till it feeles,
    Making but reservation of your selves,
    Still your owne Foes) deliver you
    As most abated Captives, to some Nation
    That wonne you without blowes, despising
    For you the City .

3   Thus I turne my backe ;
    There is a world elsewhere .

- the initial passionate attack (7/7, F #1 and the first two and a half lines of F #2, seven and a half lines in all) is heightened by four surround phrases

  " . You common cry of Curs, whose breath I hate, /As reeke a'th'rotten Fennes : . . . : I banish you, And heere remaine with your uncertaintie . /Let every feeble Rumor shake your hearts : /Your Enemies, with nodding of their Plumes/Fan you into dispaire : "

- and even when the drive of the surround phrases stops, the continuation of the onrushed F #2 condemning the Citizens to have all the 'power still/To banish your Defenders' so that these 'Curs' can become 'most abated Captives, to some Nation/That wonne you without blowes' still remains passionate (6/6, F #2's last seven lines)

- and then according to F it seems that Coriolanus finally loses self-control, for whereas most modern texts start their final sentence logically with the phrase 'despising/For you the City', relating it to how Coriolanus feels about them, F, ungrammatically in the opinion of most modern editors, sets the phrase at the end of the may-you-become-captives sequence, thus attaching it to whichever Nation that captures them, thus suggesting the captors will hate Rome because of the common folk that now dominate it

- this triggers an emotional start to his farewell, with F #3 being set as two emotional surround phrases

  " . Thus I turne my backe ; /There is a world elsewhere. "

  the emotion of the first phrase intensified by the releases (0/2)

- but, in a moment of supreme self-control, his very last words before leaving, 'There is a world elsewhere.', display enormous and perhaps surprising dignity for they are completely unembellished

The Tragedie of Anthonie and Cleopatra

Agrippa

Give me leave Cæsar ./Thou hast a Sister by the Mothers side,
between 2.2.116 - 138

Background: Anthony has returned to Rome for a meeting with
Cæsar and Lepidus to explore joining forces to deal with a possible
invasion threat from Pompey: to ease the public appearance of ten-
sion between Cæsar and Anthony, and since Anthony is now a wid-
ower following Fulvia's death, Agrippa, one of Cæsar's shrewdest
advisors, makes an audacious proposal, marriage between Anthony
and Cæsar's sister Octavia (the 'Sister' referred to in the first line)

Style: as part of a general address, initially directed towards one man

Where: a meeting place in Rome, possibly the Senate

To Whom: initially Cæsar, then Anthony in front of Lepidus, Eno-
barbus, Ventidius, and Mecenas

# of Lines: 20

Probable Timing: 1.00 minutes

Take Note: That Agrippa realises he is making a very delicate proposal can be seen not just in F #2's surround phrases in which the
names of Octavia and Anthony are first linked, but also in both
the sentence's onrush, and the fact its two lines are longer than
normal (12/13-15 syllables) – if indeed F #2 is verse, for it could
well be set as prose as is F #3, and if it is, it would suggest Agrippa
is being very careful not to draw too much attention to himself or
his proposal just yet.

Agrippa

1   Give me leave, Cæsar -

    Thou hast a sister by the mother's side,
    Admir'd Octavia.

2   Great Mark Antony
    Is now a widower {,}

    {Though} if Cleopatra heard {me, my}[reproof]
    Were well deserved of rashness.

3   To hold you in perpetual amity,
    To make your brothers, and to knit your hearts
    With an un-slipping knot, take Antony
    Octavia to his wife;   whose beauty claims
    No worse a husband [than]the best of men;
    Whose virtue, and whose general graces speak
    That which none else can utter.

4   By this marriage,
    All little jealousies, which now seem great,
    And all great fears, which now import their dangers,
    Would then be nothing.

5   [Truths] would be tales,
    Where now half tales be [truths].

6   Her love to both,
    Would each to other and all loves to both
    Draw after her.

7   Pardon what I have spoke,
    For 'tis a studied, not a present thought,
     By duty ruminated.

Agrippa

1　Give me leave Cæsar.

2　Thou hast a Sister by the Mothers side, admir'd
　　Octavia:　Great Mark Anthony is now a widdower{,}

　　{Though} if Cleopater heard {me, my}
　　[proofe] were well deserved of rashnesse .

3　To hold you in perpetuall amitie,
　　To make your Brothers, and to knit your hearts
　　With an un-slipping knot, take Anthony,
　　Octavia to his wife:　whose beauty claimes
　　No worse a husband [then] the best of men:　whose
　　Vertue, and whose generall graces, speake
　　That which none else can utter.
4　　　　　　　　　　　　　　　　　By this marriage,
　　All little Jelousies which now seeme great,
　　And all great feares, which now import their dangers,
　　Would then be nothing.
5　　　　　　　　　　　　　　[Truth's] would be tales,
　　Where now halfe tales be [truth's]:　her love to both,
　　Would each to other, and all loves to both
　　Draw after her.
6　　　　　　　　　　Pardon what I have spoke,
　　For 'tis a studied not a present thought,
　　By duty ruminated.

- the speech opens very factually, again suggesting Agrippa is being careful to let no emotion bleed into the suggestion (7/1, F's first four lines, save for the factually correct reminder to Anthony that he is a 'widdower'), and its only with the last line of F #2's sly dig about Cleopatra that the emotion intensifies (0/2)

- the actual proposal that 'to make you Brothers . . . , take Anthony,/ Octavia to his wife' is slightly passionate (1/2), while the praise of both parties, enhanced by the opening surround phrase
" : whose beauty claimes/No worse a husband then the best of men : " and the claim that the marriage would put to rest 'All little Jelousies... And all great feares' is emotional (1/5, F #3's last two and a half lines and F #4)

- and then for the last two sentences, Agrippa becomes very quiet once more, (0/1, the five lines of F #5-6), and since this starts before his F #6 apology for perhaps overstepping his authority it could well be that so far the reactions of Anthony and Cæsar (and even Octavia should she be onstage too) to Agrippa's proposal are less than encouraging

- one note: the single release in the five lines seems to be very important to Agrippa, for it underscores his reference to the hope that the 'hal- fe' truths which have plagued relationships between Octavius and Anthony to date will be eradicated by the suggested marriage, and the idea is even further heightened by being set as F #5's opening surround phrase

" . Truth's would be tales,/Where now halfe tales be truth's : "

The Tragedie of Anthonie and Cleopatra

Soothsayer

Would I had never come from {Egypt}, nor you
between 2.3.12 - 31

Background: Anthony has been manipulated into returning to
Rome for a conciliatory meeting with Cæsar and Lepidus to join
forces to deal with the threat from Pompey: during the meeting
Anthony has been further manipulated into agreeing to a marriage of convenience with Cæsar's sister Octavia as a symbol of
reconciliation (see previous speech): the following is the Egyptian
soothsayer's frank response to Anthony's blunt question, 'Now
Sirrah: you do wish your selfe in Egypt?'

Style: as part of a two handed scene

Where: unspecified, perhaps Cæsar's palace in Rome

To Whom: Anthony

# of Lines: 14

Probable Timing: 0.45 minutes

Take Note: though often regarded as a mystical character in full
control of himself and situation, here F's orthography suggests
that while the Soothsayer may start out this way, what he fears
will happen for Anthony causes him great personal problems (dis-
tress? sadness? fear?).

Soothsayer

1 Would I had never come from {Egypt}, nor you
thither .

2 But yet hie you to Egypt again.

3 O Antony, stay not by {Caesar's} side .

4 Thy daemon, [that'] thy spirit which keeps thee, is
Noble, courageous, high unmatchable,
Where Cæsar's is not ; but near him, thy angel

5 Becomes a [feared], as being o'er-powr'd : therefore
Make space enough between you .

6 If thou dost play with him at any game,
Thou art sure to lose; and of that natural luck,
He beats thee 'gainst the odds.

7   Thy lustre thickens
When he shines by .

8   I say again, thy spirit
Is all afraid to govern thee near him ;
But he [away,] 'tis noble .

Soothsayer

1   Would I had never come from {Egypt}, nor you
    thither .

2   But yet hie you to Egypt againe.

3   O Anthony) stay not by {Caesar's} side
    Thy Daemon that thy spirit which keepes thee, is
    Noble, Couragious, high unmatchable,
    Where Cæsars is not .

4   But neere him, thy Angell
    Becomes a [feare] : as being o're-powr'd, therefore
    Make space enough betweene you .

5   If thou dost play with him at any game,
    Thou art sure to loose : And of that Naturall lucke,
    He beats thee 'gainst the oddes .

6   Thy Luster thickens,
    When he shines by : I say againe, thy spirit
    Is all affraid to governe thee neere him :
    But he [alway] 'tis Noble .

• the Soothsayer's regret at having left Egypt and Anthony's ever finding his way there, plus his warning for Anthony not to stay by Cæsar's side is strongly intellectual (7/1 in the five and half lines, F #1-3)

• and his concern for Anthony seems heightened by F which sets no punctuation at the end of the Soothsayer's first line of F #3, as if the urgency of what he needs to say forces him to rush on unchecked - most modern texts remove this concern by adding a grammatically correct period

• having voiced the concern that Anthony's noble spirit will inevitably be damaged since 'Cæsars is not', as he explains how, the Soothsayer not only becomes very emotional for the rest of the speech (5/12, eight lines F #4-6), every single detail to the end of the speech is driven home by being set via eight consecutive surround phrases

The Tragedie of Cymbeline

2nd. Lord

That such a craftie Divell as is his Mother
1.6.52 - 65

Background: this less than hopeful assessment of the complete familial situation comes from one of the two Lords whose main assignation seems to be trying to keep Cloten out of the continual quarrels he tends to generate, and minimise the damages when the quarrels actually occur

Style: solo

Where: somewhere in the palace

To Whom: direct audience address

# of Lines: 14

Probable Timing: 0.45 minutes

Take Note: Presumably attendant on Clotens' every whim, and now alone, the 2nd. Lord, can express his frustration without fear of reprisal, and does so (20/20 in just fourteen lines), the relative lack of punctuation pointing much more to simple release rather than determined analysis.

2nd. Lord

1   That such a crafty devil as is his mother
    Should yield the world this ass! a woman, that
    Bears all down with her brain, and this her son
    Cannot take two from twenty, for his heart,
    And leave eighteen.

2   Alas poor Princess,
    Thou divine Imogen , what thou endur'st,
    Betwixt a father by thy step-dame govern'd,
    A mother hourly coining plots, a wooer
    More hateful [than] the foul expulsion is
    Of thy dear husband, [than] that horrid act
    Of the divorce he'ld make .

3   The heavens hold firm
    The walls of thy dear honor;   keep unshak'd
    That temple, thy fair mind, that thou mayst stand
    T'enjoy thy banish'd lord and this great land !

2nd. Lord

1   That such a craftie Divell as is his Mother
    Should yeild the world this Asse : A woman, that
    Beares all downe with her Braine, and this her Sonne,
    Cannot take two from twenty for his heart,
    And leave eighteene .

2   Alas poore Princesse,
    Thou divine Imogen , what thou endur'st,
    Betwixt a Father by thy Step-dame govern'd,
    A Mother hourely coyning plots : A Wooer,
    More hatefull [then] the foule expulsion is
    Of thy deere Husband .

3   [Then] that horrid Act
    Of the divorce, heel'd make the Heavens hold firme
    The walls of thy deere Honour .

4   Keepe unshak'd
    That Temple thy faire mind, that thou maist stand
    T'enjoy thy banish'd Lord : and this great Land .

- the occasional exasperation can be seen in the capitalised indefinite article that comes immediately after the colon both in F #1 and #2

- the first two extra breath-thoughts point to the Lord's need either to control himself and/or find the means to express his amazement as to Cloten's (mathematical) stupidity (F #1) and his presumably appalling behaviour as a 'Wooer' (F #2) , while the third, (F #3), connects two vastly disparate thoughts, pointing to a momentary loss of composure (though most modern texts regard this moment as ungrammatical and repunctuate for more rationality as shown

- given the appalling situation Britain finds itself in the play (de facto ruled by the Queene in place of the sickly and irascible Cymbeline, threatened with invasion from Italy), the final surround phrase ' : and this great Land . ' is not merely a jingoistic piece of posturing but rather points to a very determined love and concern for the country

BIBLIOGRAPHY

AND

APPENDICES

BIBLIOGRAPHY

The most easily accessible general information is to be found under the citations of *Campbell*, and of *Halliday*. The finest summation of matters academic is to be found within the all-encompassing *A Textual Companion*, listed below in the first part of the bibliography under *Wells, Stanley and Taylor, Gary* (eds.)

Individual modem editions consulted are listed below under the separate headings 'The Complete Works in Compendium Format' and 'The Complete Works in Separate Individual Volumes,' from which the modem text audition speeches have been collated and compiled.

All modem act, scene, and/or line numbers refer the reader to *The Riverside Shakespeare,* in my opinion still the best of the complete works, despite the excellent compendiums that have been published since.

The F/Q material is taken from a variety of already published sources, including not only all the texts listed in the 'Photostatted Reproductions in Compendium Format' below, but also earlier individually printed volumes, such as the twentieth century editions published under the collective title *The Facsimiles of Plays from The First Folio of Shakespeare* by Faber & Gwyer, and the nineteenth century editions published on behalf of The New Shakespere Society.

The heading 'Single Volumes of Special Interest' is offered to newcomers to Shakespeare in the hope that the books may add useful knowledge about the background and craft of this most fascinating of theatrical figures.

PHOTOSTATTED REPRODUCTIONS OF THE ORIGINAL TEXTS IN COMPENDIUM FORMAT

Allen, M.J.B. and K. Muir, (eds.). *Shakespeare's Plays in Quarto.* Berkeley: University of California Press, 1981.

Blaney, Peter (ed.). *The Norton Facsimile (The First Folio of Shakespeare).* New York: W.W.Norton & Co., Inc., 1996 (see also Hinman, below).

Brewer D.S. (ed.). *Mr. William Shakespeare's Comedies, Histories & Tragedies, The Second/Third/Fourth Folio Reproduced in Facsimile.* (3 vols.), 1983.

Hinman, Charlton (ed.). *The Norton Facsimile (The First Folio of Shake-speare)*. New York: W.W.Norton & Company, Inc., 1968.

Kokeritz, Helge (ed.). *Mr. William Shakespeare 's Comedies, Histories & Tragedies*. New Haven: Yale University Press, 1954.

Moston, Doug (ed.). *Mr. William Shakespeare's Comedies, Histories, and Tragedies*. New York: Routledge, 1998.

MODERN TYPE VERSION OF THE FIRST FOLIO IN COMPENDIUM FORMAT

Freeman, Neil. (ed.). *The Applause First Folio of Shakespeare in Modern Type*. New York & London: Applause Books, 2001.

MODERN TEXT VERSIONS OF THE COMPLETE WORKS IN COMPENDIUM FORMAT

Craig, H. and D. Bevington (eds.). *The Complete Works of Shakespeare*. Glenview: Scott, Foresman and Company, 1973.

Evans, G.B. (ed.). *The Riverside Shakespeare*. Boston: Houghton Mifflin Company, 1974.

Wells, Stanley and Gary Taylor (eds.). *The Oxford Shakespeare, William Shakespeare , the Complete Works, Original Spelling Edition,* Oxford: The Clarendon Press, 1986.

Wells, Stanley and Gary Taylor (eds.). *The Oxford Shakespeare, William Shakespeare, The Complete Works, Modern Spelling Edition.* Oxford: The Clarendon Press, 1986.

MODERN TEXT VERSIONS OF THE COMPLETE WORKS IN SEPARATE INDIVIDUAL VOLUMES

The Arden Shakespeare. London: Methuen & Co. Ltd., Various dates, editions, and editors .

Folio Texts. Freeman, Neil H. M. (ed.) Applause First Folio Editions, 1997, and following.

The New Cambridge Shakespeare. Cambridge: Cambridge University Press. Various dates, editions, and editors.

New Variorum Editions of Shakespeare. Furness, Horace Howard (original editor.). New York: 1880, Various reprints. All these volumes have been in a state of re-editing and reprinting since they first appeared in 1880. Various dates, editions, and editors.

The Oxford Shakespeare. Wells, Stanley (general editor). Oxford: Oxford University Press, Various dates and editors.

The New Penguin Shakespeare . Harmondsworth, Middlesex: Penguin Books, Various dates and editors.

The Shakespeare Globe Acting Edition. Tucker, Patrick and Holden, Michael. (eds.). London: M.H.Publications, Various dates.

SINGLE VOLUMES OF SPECIAL INTEREST

Baldwin, T.W. *William Shakespeare's Petty School.* 1943.

Baldwin, T.W. *William Shakespeare's Small wtin and Lesse Greeke.* (2 vols.) 1944.

Barton, John. *Playing Shakespeare.* 1984.

Beckerman, Bernard. *Shakespeare at the Globe, I 599-1609.* 1962. Berryman, John. *Berryman 's Shakespeare.* 1999.

Bloom, Harold. *Shakespeare: The Invention of the Human.* 1998. Booth, Stephen (ed.). *Shakespeare's Sonnets.* 1977.

Briggs, Katharine. *An Encyclopedia of Fairies.* 1976.

Campbell, Oscar James, and Edward G. Quinn (eds.). *The Reader's Encyclopedia of Shakespeare. 1966.*

Crystal, David, and Ben Crystal. *Shakespeare's Words: A Glossary & Language Companion.* 2002.

Flatter, Richard. *Shakespeare's Producing Hand.* 1948 (reprint).

Ford, Boris. (ed.). *The Age of Shakespeare.* 1955.

Freeman, Neil H.M. *Shakespeare's First Texts.* 1994.

Greg, W.W. *The Editorial Problem in Shakespeare: A Survey of the Foundations of the Text.* 1954 (3rd. edition).

Gurr, Andrew . *Playgoing in Shakespeare's London.* 1987. Gurr, Andrew. *The Shakespearean Stage, 1574-1642.* 1987. Halliday, F.E. *A Shakespeare Companion.* 1952.

Harbage, Alfred. *Shakespeare's Audience.* 1941.

Harrison, G.B. (ed.). *The Elizabethan Journals.* 1965 (revised, 2 vols.).

Harrison, G.B. (ed.). *A Jacobean Journal.* 1941.

Harrison, G.B. (ed.). *A Second Jacobean Journal.* 1958.

Hinman, Charlton. *The Printing and Proof Reading of the First Folio of Shakespeare.* 1963 (2 vols.).

Joseph, Bertram. *Acting Shakespeare.* 1960.

Joseph, Miriam (Sister). *Shakespeare's Use of The Arts of wnguage.* 1947.

King, T.J. *Casting Shakespeare's Plays.* 1992.

Lee, Sidney and C.T. Onions. *Shakespeare's England : An Account Of The Life And Manners Of His Age.* (2 vols.) 1916.

Linklater, Kristin. *Freeing Shakespeare's Voice*. 1992.

Mahood, **M .M**. *Shakespeare's Wordplay*. 1957.

O'Connor, Gary. *William Shakespeare: A Popular Life*. 2000.

Ordish, T.F. *Early London Theatres*. 1894. (1971 reprint).

Rodenberg, Patsy. *Speaking Shakespeare*. 2002.

Schoenbaum. S. *William Shakespeare: A Documentary Life*. 1975.

Shapiro, Michael. *Children of the Revels*. 1977.

Simpson, Percy. *Shakespeare's Punctuation*. 1969 (reprint).

Smith, Irwin. *Shakespeare's Blackfriars Playhouse* . 1964.

Southern, Richard. *The Staging of Plays Before Shakespeare*. 1973.

Spevack, M. *A Complete and Systematic Concordance to the Works Of Shakespeare* . 1968-1980 (9vols.).

Tillyard, E.M.W. *The Elizabethan World Picture*. 1942.

Trevelyan, G.M. (ed.). *Illustrated English Social History*. 1942.

Vendler, Helen. *The Art of Shakespeare's Sonnets*. 1999.

Walker, Alice F. *Textual Problems of the First Folio*. 1953.

Walton, J.K. *The Quarto Copy of the First Folio*. 1971.

Warren, Michael. *William Shakespeare, The Parallel King Lear 1608-1623*.

Wells, Stanley and Taylor, Gary (eds.). *Modernising Shakespeare's Spelling, with Three Studies in The Text of Henry V.* 1975.

Wells, Stanley. *Re-Editing Shakespeare for the Modern Reader.* 1984.

Wells, Stanley and Gary Taylor (eds.). *William Shakespeare: A Textual Companion* . 1987.

Wright, George T. *Shakespeare's Metrical Art*. 1988.

HISTORICAL DOCUMENTS

Daniel, Samuel. *The Fowre Bookes of the Civile Warres Between The Howses Of Lancaster and Yorke*. 1595.

Holinshed, Raphael. *Chronicles of England, Scotland and Ireland*. 1587 (2nd. edition).

Halle, Edward. *The Union of the Two Noble and Illustre Famelies of Lancastre And Yorke*. 1548 (2nd. edition).

Henslowe, Philip: Foakes, R.A. and Rickert (eds.). *Henslowe's Diary*. 1961.

Plutarch: North, Sir Thomas (translation of a work in French prepared by Jacques Amyots). *The Lives of The Noble Grecians and Romanes*. 1579.

APPENDIX 1:
GUIDE TO THE EARLY TEXTS

A QUARTO (Q)

A single text, so called because of the book size resulting from a particular method of printing. Eighteen of Shakespeare's plays were published in this format by different publishers at various dates between 1594-1622, prior to the appearance of the 1623 Folio.

THE FIRST FOLIO (F1)'

Thirty-six of Shakespeare's plays (excluding *Pericles* and *Two Noble Kinsmen,* in which he had a hand) appeared in one volume, published in 1623. All books of this size were termed Folios, again because of the sheet size and printing method, hence this volume is referred to as the First Folio. For publishing details see Bibliography, 'Photostated Reproductions of the Original Texts.'

THE SECOND FOLIO (F2)

Scholars suggest that the Second Folio, dated 1632 but perhaps not published until 1640, has little authority, especially since it created hundreds of new problematic readings of its own. Nevertheless more than 800 modern text readings can be attributed to it. The **Third Folio** (1664) and the **Fourth Folio** (1685) have even less authority, and are rarely consulted except in cases of extreme difficulty.

APPENDIX 2:
WORD, WORDS, WORDS

PART ONE: VERBAL CONVENTIONS (AND HOW THEY WILL BE SET IN THE FOLIO TEXT)

"THEN" AND "THAN"

These two words, though their neutral vowels sound different to modern ears, were almost identical to Elizabethan speakers and readers, despite their different meanings. F and Q make little distinction between them, setting them interchangeably . The original setting will be used, and the modern reader should soon get used to substituting one for the other as necessary.

"I," "AY," AND "AYE"

F/Q often print the personal pronoun "I" and the word of agreement "aye" simply as "I." Again, the modern reader should quickly get used to this and make the substitution when necess ary. The reader should also be aware that very occasionally either word could be used and the phrase make perfect sense, even though different meanings would be implied.

"MY SELFE/HIM SELFE/HER SELFE" VERSUS "MYSELF/HIMSELF/HER-SELF"

Generally F/Q separate the two parts of the word, "my selfe" while most modern texts set the single word "myself." The difference is vital, based on Elizabethan philosophy. Elizabethans regarded themselves as composed of two parts, the corporeal "I," and the more spiritual part, the "self." Thus, when an Elizabethan character refers to "my selfe," he or she is often referring to what is to all intents and purposes a separate being, even if that being is a particular part of him- or herself. Thus soliloquies can be thought of as a debate between the "I" and "my selfe," and, in such speeches, even though there may be only one character on-stage, it's as if there were two distinct entities present.

UNUSUAL SPELLING OF REAL NAMES, BOTH OF PEOPLE AND PLACES

Real names, both of people and places, and foreign languages are often reworked for modern understanding. For example, the French town often set in Fl as "Callice" is usually reset as "Calais." F will be set as is.

NON-GRAMMATICAL USES OF VERBS IN BOTH TENSE AND APPLICATION

Modern texts 'correct' the occasional Elizabethan practice of setting a singular noun with plural verb (and vice versa), as well as the infrequent use of the past tense of a verb to describe a current situation. The F reading will be set as is, without annotation.

ALTERNATIVE SETTINGS OF A WORD WHERE DIFFERENT SPELLINGS MAINTAIN THE SAME MEANING

F/Q occasionally set what appears to modern eyes as an archaic spelling of a word for which there is a more common modern alternative, for example "murther" for murder , "burthen" for burden, "moe" for more, "vilde" for vile. Though some modern texts set the Fl (or alternative Q) setting, others modernise. Fl will be set as is with no annotation.

ALTERNATIVE SETTINGS OF A WORD WHERE DIFFERENT SPELLINGS SUGGEST DIFFERENT MEANINGS

Far more complicated is the situation where, while an Elizabethan could substitute one word formation for another and still imply the same thing, to modern eyes the substituted word has an entirely different meaning to the one it has replaced. The following is by no means an exclusive list of the more common dual-spelling, dual-meaning words

anticke-antique	mad-made	sprite-spirit
born-borne	metal-mettle	sun-sonne
hart-heart	mote-moth	travel-travaill
human-humane	pour-(po wre)-power	through-thorough
lest-least	reverent-reverend	troth-truth
lose-loose	right-rite	whether-whither

Some of these doubles offer a metrical problem too, for example "sprite," a one syllable word, versus "spirit." A potential problem occurs in *A Midsummer Nights Dream,* where the modern text s set Q1's "thorough," and thus the scansion pattern of elegant magic can be established, whereas F1's more plebeian "through" sets up a much more awkward and clumsy moment.

The F reading will be set in the Folio Text, as will the modern texts' substitution of a different word formation in the Modern Text. If the modern text substitution has the potential to alter the meaning (and sometimes scansion) of the line, it will be noted accordingly.

PART TWO: WORD FORMATIONS COUNTED AS EQUIVALENTS FOR THE FOLLOWING SPEECHES

Often the spelling differences between the original and modern texts are quite obvious, as with "she"/"shee". And sometimes Folio text passages are so flooded with longer (and sometimes shorter) spellings that, as described in the General Introduction, it would seem that vocally something unusual is taking place as the character speaks.

However, there are some words where the spelling differences are so marginal that they need not be explored any further. The following is by no mean s an exclusive list of word s that in the main will not be taken into account when discussing emotional moments in the various commentaries accompanying the audition speeches.

(modern text spelling shown first)

and- &	murder - murther	tabor - taber
apparent - apparant	mutinous - mutenous	ta'en - tane
briars - briers	naught - nought	then - than
choice - choise	obey - obay	theater - theatre
defense - defence	o'er - o're	uncurrant - uncurrent
debtor - debter	offense - offence	than - then
enchant - inchant	quaint - queint	venomous - venemous
endurance - indurance	reside - recide	virtue - vertue
ere - e'er	Saint - S.	weight - waight
expense - expence	sense - sence	
has - ha's	sepulchre - sepulcher	
heinous - hainous	show - shew	
I'11 - Ile	solicitor - soliciter	
increase - encrease	sugar - suger	

Appendix 2

APPENDIX 3:
THE PATTERN OF MAGIC, RITUAL &
INCANTATION

THE PATTERNS OF "NORMAL" CONVERSATION

The normal pattern of a regular Shakespearean verse line is akin to five pairs of human heart beats, with ten syllables being arranged in five pairs of beats, each pair alternating a pattern of a weak stress followed by a strong stress. Thus, a normal ten syllable heartbeat line (with the emphasis on the capitalised words) would read as

weak- STRONG, weak - STRONG, weak- STRONG, weak- STRONG, weak- STRONG
(shall I com- PARE thee TO a SUMM- ers DAY)

Breaks would either be in length (under or over ten syllables) or in rhythm (any combinations of stresses other than the five pairs of weak-strong as shown above), or both together.

THE PATTERNS OF MAGIC, RITUAL, AND INCANTATION

Whenever magic is used in the Shakespeare plays the form of the spoken verse changes markedly in two ways. The length is usually reduced from ten to just seven syllables, and the pattern of stresses is completely reversed, as if the heartbeat was being forced either by the circumstances of the scene or by the need of the speaker to completely change direction. Thus in comparison to the normal line shown above, or even the occasional minor break, the more tortured and even dangerous magic or ritual line would read as

STRONG - weak, STRONG- weak, STRONG - weak, STRONG
(WHEN shall WE three MEET a GAINE)

The strain would be even more severely felt in an extended passage, as when the three weyward Sisters begin the potion that will fetch Macbeth to them. Again, the spoken emphasis is on the capitalised words and the effort of, and/or fixed determination in, speaking can clearly be felt.

> THRICE the BRINDed CAT hath MEW"D
> THRICE and ONCE the HEDGE-Pigge WHIN"D
> HARPier CRIES, 'tis TIME, 'tis TIME.

UNUSUAL ASPECTS OF MAGIC

It's not always easy for the characters to maintain it. And the magic doesn't always come when the character expects it. What is even more interesting is that while the pattern is found a lot in the Comedies, it is usually in much gentler situations, often in songs *(Two Gentlemen of Verona, Merry Wives of Windsor, Much Ado About Nothing, Twelfth Night, The Winters Tale)* and/or simplistic poetry *(Loves Labours Lost* and *As You Like It),* as well as the casket sequence in *The Merchant of Venice.*

It's too easy to dismiss these settings as inferior poetry known as doggerel. But this may be doing the moment and the character a great disservice. The language may be simplistic, but the passion and the magical/ritual intent behind it is wonderfully sincere. It's not just a matter of magic for the sake of magic, as with Pucke and Oberon enchanting mortals and Titania. It's a matter of the human heart's desires too. Orlando, in *As You Like It,* when writing peons of praise to Rosalind suggesting that she is composed of the best parts of the mythical heroines because

> THEREfore HEAVen NATure CHARG"D
> THAT one BODie SHOULD be FILL"D
> WITH all GRACes WIDE enLARG"D

And what could be better than Autolycus *(The Winters Tale)* using magic in his opening song as an extra enticement to trap the unwary into buying all his peddler's goods, ballads, and trinkets.

To help the reader, most magic/ritual lines will be bolded in the Folio text version of the speeches.

ACKNOWLEDGMENTS

Neil dedicated *The Applause First Folio in Modern Type*
        "To All Who Have Gone Before"
and there are so many who have gone before in the sharing of Shakespeare through publication. Back to John Heminge and Henry Condell who published *Mr. William Shakespeares Comedies, Histories, & Tragedies* which we now know as The First Folio and so preserved 18 plays of Shakespeare which might otherwise have been lost. As they wrote in their note "To the great Variety of Readers.":

> Reade him, therefore; and againe, and againe : And if then you doe not like him, surely you are in some manifest danger, not to understand him. And so we leave you to other of his Friends, whom if you need, can be your guides: if you neede them not, you can lead yourselves, and others, and such readers we wish him.

I want to thank John Cerullo for believing in these books and helping to spread Neil's vision. I want to thank Rachel Reiss for her invaluable advice and assistance. I want to thank my wife, Maren and my family for giving me support, but above all I want to thank Julie Stockton, Neil's widow, who was able to retrive Neil's files from his old non-internet connected Mac, without which these books would not be possible. Thank you Julie.

Shakespeare for Everyone!

Paul Sugarman, April 2021

AUTHOR BIOS

Neil Freeman (1941-2015) trained as an actor at the Bristol Old Vic Theatre School. In the world of professional Shakespeare he acted in fourteen of the plays, directed twenty-four, and coached them all many times over.

His groundbreaking work in using the first printings of the Shakespeare texts in performance, on the rehearsal floor and in the classroom led to lectures at the Shakespeare Association of America and workshops at both the ATHE and VASTA, and grants/fellowships from the National Endowment for the Arts (USA), The Social Science and Humanities Research Council (Canada), and York University in Toronto. He prepared and annotated the thirty-six individual Applause First Folio editions of Shakespeare's plays and the complete *The Applause First Folio of Shakespeare in Modern Type*. For Applause he also compiled *Once More Unto the Speech, Dear Friends*, three volumes (Comedy, History and Tragedy) of Shakespeare speeches with commentary and insights to inform audition preparation.

He was Professor Emeritus in the Department of Theatre, Film and Creative Writing at the University of British Columbia, and dramaturg with The Savage God project, both in Vancouver, Canada. He also taught regularly at the National Theatre School of Canada, Concordia University, Brigham Young University.. He had a Founder's Ring (and the position of Master Teacher) with Shakespeare & Company in Lenox, Mass: he was associated with the Will Geer Theatre in Los Angeles; Bard on the Beach in Vancouver; Repercussion Theatre in Montreal; and worked with the Stratford Festival, Canada, and Shakespeare Santa Cruz.

Paul Sugarman is an actor, editor, writer, and teacher of Shakespeare. He is founder of the Instant Shakespeare Company, which has presented annual readings of all of Shakespeare's plays in New York City for over twenty years. For Applause Theatre & Cinema Books, he edited John Russell Brown's publication of *Shakescenes: Shakespeare for Two* and The Applause Shakespeare Library, as well as Neil Freeman's Applause First Folio Editions and *The Applause First Folio of Shakespeare in Modern Type*. He has published pocket editions of all of Shakespeare's plays using the original settings of the First Folio in modern type for Puck Press. Sugarman studied with Kristin Linklater and Tina Packer at Shakespeare & Company where he met Neil Freeman.